G.

# RAILWAY RELICS

# RAILWAY RELICS

Bryan Morgan

LONDON

IAN ALLAN

First published 1969

SBN 7110 0092 1



*Published by Ian Allan Ltd, Shepperton, Surrey, and printed in the United Kingdom by The Press at Coombelands Ltd, Addlestone, Weybridge, Surrey.* 624/DXX/769

# *CONTENTS*

Acknowledgements 6

Introduction 8

*PART ONE: The Tramway Age*

I: Prelude 13
II: Tramways, 1750-1800 19
III: Tramways, 1800–1830 27

*PART TWO: The Railway Scene*

IV: Transition 45
V: Civil Engineering 49
VI: Stations and Their Architecture 63

*PART THREE: Locomotion*

VII: Engines on Ice 76
VIII: Still in Steam 90
IX: Carriages and Caterpillars 108

Miscellany 115

Gazetteer 118

List of Engineers, Architects, etc. 128

"*In my Eden, we have a few beam-engines, saddle-tank locomotives, overshot water-wheels and other beautiful pieces of obsolete machinery to play with . . .*"

W. H. Auden: *Vespers*

## *ACKNOWLEDGEMENTS*

BEFORE starting work on this book I recognised that, if it were to have any claims to accuracy and completeness, it would rely heavily on the enthusiasm and experience of Britain's railway-lovers and local historians. In the event I have been fortunate enough to find advisers in many parts of the British Isles and with interests in varied facets of the railway scene. Other local information has been kindly supplied by the chief librarians, town clerks, museum curators, etc., of the following cities, towns and boroughs: Birmingham, Brighton, Bristol, Caernarvon, Canterbury, Coventry, Croydon, Edinburgh, Glasgow, Leicester, Liverpool, Manchester, Neath, Newcastle, Stoke, Tiverton and Wantage: of the county of Staffordshire and of the Science Museum, S. Kensington, London.

I have also received the aid of several departments of British Railways, including those of the press and public relations officers of the various regions (particularly the LMR) and of the BRB itself as well as that of the curator of historical relics, whose staff have given me much of their time. I would in particular like to stress that, though in these pages I have had to draw attention to what I consider ill-advised and even anti-social decisions made by recent BR Boards acting under political pressure, I have received only interest and help from the officers of that complex. All views expressed or implied in this book are, of course, personal ones.

Chapter VII has drawn heavily on advice from the secretaries or other officers of the flourishing group of private preservation organisations, and in particular those of the: Bluebell RPS, Bulleid Pacific RS, Dart Valley R, Festiniog RS, Foxfield Lt. RS, Keighley & Worth Valley RS, Kent & E. Sussex RA, London RPS, Merchant Navy Loco. PS, 1758 Middleton RT, Midland & Gt. Northern Jt. RS, Narrow Gauge RMT, Scottish RPS, Severn Valley RS, Snowdon Mountain R and Talyllyn RC.

Of other corporate bodies who have aided I would like to single out the Railway and Canal Historical Society, the Association of Railway Preservation Societies and the Victorian Society. Further organisations which have helped me include: Allied Ironfounders Ltd, Butlin's Ltd, David & Charles Ltd, The Dinorwic Slate Quarries Ltd, London Transport, The National Coal Board, The National Trust and *The Railway Magazine*.

The list of individual advisers is a long one. Some are officers of the groups mentioned above whom I have troubled with lengthy correspondence, others have helped by supplying single—but most important—data, while others again have held a general 'watching brief' throughout the assembly of this book. It would, however, be invidious to list them other than in the mainly alphabetical order which follows: Capt. P. Manisty, Dr. R. and Mrs. S. Youell, Dr. M. Lewis, Dr. A. Pacey, Rev. E. Boston, Mrs. J. Fawcett, and B. Alexander, J. Ashdown, O. Ashmore, A. Brewster, J. Bushell, P. Carter, H. Casserley, J. Coop, M. Crew, R. Davies, H. Denton, N. Evans, J. Fairbrother, P. Gibbons, M. Haddon, I. Harris, J. Harris, H. Kingsbury, A. Lambert, J. Latham, C. Lee, D. Lloyd, R. Nichol, H. Oliver, H. Paar, A. Pope, J. Price, G. Rattenbury, D. Sheldon, D. Shepherd, R. Smith, P. Stevens, H. Street, W. Tharby, C. Townley, J. True, F. Turton, J. White, and R. Wildman Esquires.

This book is not one of primary research, and has hence drawn heavily on material both generally and privately published. In particular—and for want of a formal bibliography which would, of course, include several standard railway reference works—I would like here to recognise the help rendered by the writers cited in the text. The works of David Walters (bridges), Alan Blower (tunnels), David Lloyd (stations) and H. C. Casserley and John True with their invaluable stock-listing on the locomotive side have proved especially useful. Needless to say, the author takes full responsibility for the errors which will inevitably have slipped into print despite the efforts of so large and well-informed a panel of consultants.

Photographic credits are due to all regions of British Railways and to the Board's department of historical relics; to British Insulated Callenders Cables, Holman Brothers, London Transport and the National Coal Board; to the City of Birmingham Museum, the Museum of Science and Engineering, Newcastle, the Royal Scottish Museum, Edinburgh, and the Shakespeare Birthplace Trust; to the Bluebell Archives, the Dart Valley Railway Co, the Festiniog Railway Society, the Foxfield Light Railway Society, the Middleton Railway Trust, the Talyllyn Railway Co, and the Narrow Gauge Museum, Towyn, and to the undermentioned individuals, some of whom have unfortunately proved impossible to trace:

B. Ashworth, Rev. E. Boston, I. Carr, H. Casserley, J. Clarke, A. Cox, H. Denton, P. Edmonds, P. Gerald, R. Hall, I. Holt, G. King, C. Loftus, R. Marshall, W. Mitchell, J. Price, P. Ransome-Wallis, R. Read, P. Riley, J. Scrace, W. Tharby, J. Vaughan, A. Vickers, R. Vincent, V. Wake, C. Walker, D. Walters, G. Wheeler and C. Whitehouse. Particular thanks are tendered to the bodies and individuals who, in the interests of historical completeness, have given permission to reproduce *gratis*.

B. M., April 1969

# *INTRODUCTION*

A GENERATION ago, the term 'industrial archaeology' had hardly a meaning: today it forms the basis of professorial chairs, curatorships, publishers' series and all the apparatus of professional scholarship as well as a lively interest for thousands of informed amateurs. For this upsurge to take place at all perhaps demanded the social revolution of recent decades. That it has taken the form which it has must be attributed largely to two complementary factors—a negative revulsion from the anonymous technology and architecture of the present, and a positive appreciation of the craftsmanship of the age of an earlier unfought revolution. Today, when a gas turbine looks like an alternator looks like a space-rocket looks like a metal cylinder, and when an office looks like a station looks like an hotel looks like a glass tower, the period from (say) 1760 to 1914 appears a last, golden age of functional and comprehensible design.

Yet none of the technologies of this recent yet remote past have so much fascination for the non-specialist as that of its railways. A forge hammer, a pumping engine, even a canal lock—these exist in their own worlds, and though the non-specialist may admire their workmanship their purpose is at a remove from him. But for nearly two centuries the public has regarded railways, with all their glories and eccentricities, as in a sense *theirs*. The openings of early nineteenth-century tramways, for instance, were saluted with guns, bells, balls, banquets and five-hour speeches in a fashion rarely accorded to new pits and harbours. And well over a century ago, in the aftermath of the Great Exhibition, at a time when it was almost a Fortieth Article that the world (and in particular, Britain) got better for ever, the locomotives of a previous generation were being deliberately preserved for a blend of reasons—technical curiosity, affection, and even a kind of gratitude.

This attitude to the railway past is not confined to Britain. Even in Spain, for instance, there is a mock-up, pleasure-park kind of railway running under the slogan 'Travel as they did in grandfather's day'—for all the world as if this were not what one did most of the time on Spanish main lines. But quite apart from the peculiar sentiments which they engender in the British breast (a locomotive, Fanny Kemble felt in 1830, was second only to a horse as a pattable object) and their equation with childhood holidays and adult moments of decision or escape, we have more excuse than most nations to be grateful for what Trevelyan called 'Britain's great gift to the world'. We can look back with not merely nostalgia but pride to the invention on which, above all others, a unique century of history was built.

This attitude may have changed fifty years hence, when only the old will remember the serious use of steam locomotives and even tracks as we know them may have given way to some concrete contraption; but at the moment we are in an intermediate phase where the original face of our railway system is still discernable under the cosmetic dressing of later ages. At this moment too not all our leisure is spent between the TV screen and the trailer speedboat, not all our efforts to escape from the contemporary agony take the form of wearing fancy dress and deafening ourselves at the juke-box. As the British railway system contracts, ever more time is spent on studying, photographing, writing-up, tape-recording and—most important of all—physically preserving the relics of its past.

This movement began in gloriously English fashion with the amateurs—young and impoverished ones for the most part—who, when even the Science Museum was short on railway exhibits and Clapham meant no more to railway-lovers than the site of the world's busiest junction, were uprooting trees in North Wales and ferrying trams across the Irish Sea. In their wake have followed the doctors and the dons with their monographs and reference collections: in particular, one should be grateful to Jack Simmons for bringing to transport history the highest standards of the professional and professorial historian. It is in many ways admirable that there should be this wide spread of interest devoted to the preservation of railway relics—on their original sites wherever possible, and where not, in museum collections. But the multiplicity of bodies now involved (there is not, of course, one 'British Railway Preservation Society': there are at least a hundred in the field, all with more or less specialised interests) leads to two difficulties.

One of these is political: is a fish-bellied rail of 1810 which would rust away if left *in situ*, or a narrow-gauge locomotive which is no longer steamable, better housed in a museum of local antiquities (which may be inaccessable and able to open for only a few hours a week) or in a central national collection of transport material? There are arguments for and against both approaches, though they cannot be set out here. But, *given* the wide geographical spread of Britain's railway antiquities preserved in museums as well as on their original sites, how is an interested party to locate those of special concern to him, be certain that they are still where he believes they are, and link them to allied survivors?

This book has been compiled as an attempt to answer that second question. Although it follows a broadly chronological flow it is in no sense a railway history; and although it concludes with a topographical index it is by no means a simple gazetteer. It is hoped that this compromise approach will enable knowledgeable readers specialising in a particular aspect of the railway scene (or a particular region) to locate material of special interest to them, whilst at the same time presenting an outline of that scene as a whole for the benefit of the non-specialist—and, in particular, for the overseas visitor. The latter may appreciate being reminded here that many British museums close on Sundays, but a few on Mondays instead, and that the season for open-air attractions generally runs from Easter to late September. Entrance to civic museums and general collections is generally free: for more specialised attractions, tolls are charged.

The book has divided itself, rather than been divided, into three parts. The first section, on railways before 1830, was originally conceived as a single chapter, and the author recognises that some enthusiasts may resent the space which it has now been given. But recent years have seen a great increase of interest in the pre-history of railways and an immense amount of work (nearly all of it, again, carried out by amateur experts) devoted to locating and dating the traces of this period and attempting to preserve them from the cancers of motorways and 'development areas'.

One outcome of this activity was the late Bertram Baxter's *Stone Blocks and Iron Rails*. To anyone who knows that book, the debt owed by the early chapters of the present one is obvious. Even allowing for a difference of approach, Baxter has not been slavishly followed in the present work, and advantage has been taken of more recent information wherever available. But it is largely due to his life's work that the claim can be made that every major surviving work of the industrial tramway age—and the bulk of minor ones—is mentioned here.

The second section is concerned with the more static aspects of the railway age proper, with its civil engineering and its stations. Even apart from the fact that (for want of an adequate definition of industrial archaeology itself) there is no recognised *terminus ad quem* here, no date after which a railway relic ceases to be historic, this selection must be representative rather than comprehensive and thin out with the passing of decades rather than come to a fixed end in time. Well over 100,000 railway structures still survive from the last century, and this book was never conceived as a list of dead lines and abandoned bridges. On the contrary, it can be taken that the buildings mentioned in these chapters are used for passenger traffic unless there is a note to the contrary, and that with a few minor exceptions the plates show 'as at now' views. Particularly with regard to stations, the 'exhibits' have hence been chosen on a balance of intrinsic importance and of representing the first (or best) survivor of a school. But since the selections are at least more than personal, and wherever possible have been based on a consensus of expert opinion, it is hoped that this second section will do more than serve as a guide to the relics of today and will play a part in ensuring their preservation. The works of the railway age were built just after the date at which (according to certain official prejudices) worthy additions continued to be made to the English scene; and despite the recent awakening of public taste, the many (and sometimes government-recognised) bodies interested in the preservation of later buildings have proved almost toothless against the host of forces making for the destruction of our environment. The more widely these irreplaceable national assets are publicised, the more hope there is of the maximum salvage from the wreck.

The final section of the text includes a still more arbitrary miscellany of *objets*, opening with a few pages at the beginning of chapter VI which should perhaps be read at this stage by those who regard 'Britain's railways' as synonymous with 'British Railways'. But the bulk of it is dedicated to what for many readers will be the exemplar of the national railway past, the steam locomotive. Here the time-scale is different again, for with the passing of the last plume of steam on the country's main lines even a still-active GWR 0–6–0PT becomes a rare jewel. As these chapters show, however, there is still a wide representation of steam in Britain for those prepared to look for it.

So much for the contents of this book: certain omissions must now be noted. BR, reasonably enough, formally differentiates between 'relics' and 'records'; and the present selection of survivors is still more rigorous in that it excludes not only all paperwork (including posters, handbills, advertisements, tickets, timetables, maps and all inflamatory material WHATSOEVER) but also a range of seals, detached insignia and even signboards. Another important omission is of almost anything which smells of the replica, the reconstruction or the model. Certain gaps in railway history (particularly in the motive power department) can only be filled by serious examples of the modeller's art; and on a more trivial level one prizes—for instance—that house-that-Jack-built which the diligent can still study at Clapham, the electroplated coffee-urn in the shape of a broad-gauge locomotive which made the coffee which disgusted Brunel in the 1840s. But such do not belong here.

Also excluded are almost all sites, sentimentalities, statues and shrines. *L'ingenieur* Locke below his viaduct on a dirt-road in Normandy, Murray at Leeds, even the tomb of Stephenson beside Telford's in Westminster Abbey—these too are part of the railway scene, but are no more part of the scene of this book than are such more humble souvenirs as locomotive name-plates and whistles. And finally, since this book is restricted to objects made for the mainland of Britain and preserved there (with even the north and south of Ireland and the Isle of Man receiving no more than marginal attention), it should be mentioned that Douglas, IoM, is the centre of a very lively narrow-gauge steam railway whose locomotives date back to 1873 as well as of two interesting tramways. Steam has virtually vanished from every part of Ireland; but there are important railway exhibits, including several locomotives, in the Belfast museum, and up to a dozen engines are preserved at other sites in both the north and the republic. Local associations include the Railway Preservation Society of Ireland (22 Kensington Park, Bangor, Co. Down).

Yet the most important caveats of all must be to the effect that this *is* the first compendium of its kind and not the tenth edition of a year-book. Despite the advice of the correspondents so inadequately thanked above, and continual up-dating in the preparatory stages, it is unlikely that even as written these pages escaped the plague or errors endemic to railway books; and in the months occupied by publication the scene will have changed again. A few more BR lines will have been closed, their stations razed and their iron bridges dismantled; on the credit side a further length of stone-blocked track will have been unearthed with rails intact and another preservation society will be at work in a disused quarry.

And all the time, too, locomotives are being newly housed and the smaller railway exhibits moved within museums from reserve collections to display cases and back or loaned around the country, so that even where these more fossilised exhibits are concerned information dates swiftly. Perhaps rightly, the transport relics which have survived the shipwrecks of time are themselves not static things but to a large extent still in a state of mobility.

This book is hence not presented as a definitive catalogue, but rather as an entry into a complex field. If in future editions a few sins of ommission are corrected, a few important omissions are made good, and a more reliable guide is presented to a changing world, then it will be due to the labours of one group of men and women. They are those who have made the present essay possible, who are not merely invited but pleaded with to address their comments to its author, and to whom it is here informally dedicated: the railway historians of Britain.

PART ONE

# *THE TRAMWAY AGE*

## *I PRELUDE*

THE GREAT and ancient monuments of the world—the Wall of China, the Pyramids, Stonehenge—could be built only by the transportation of stone blocks on rollers, sleds and eventually (and at an unknown date) wheeled vehicles. The last two of these methods would have left score-marks on suitable soil; and any farm-track today demonstrates that, once a vehicle has begun to cut parallel lines along a regularly-worked route, it tends to follow and deepen them. It creates a *railway* in the most primitive sense of a track affording guidance and an element (though in these examples a small element) of frictional reduction.

If only through the impermanence of their substrates, no certain traces of proto-railways of this antiquity remain. But in classical times paved thoroughfares were common, and archaeologists seem agreed that the wheel-ruts found in Roman pavements were consciously adopted as guide-ways for wagons even though their origin may have been accidental. According to some authorities such grooves were deliberately cut into the streets of Syracuse and perhaps Malta in neolithic times, whilst other writers see a reminiscence of them in the longitudinal stone slabs set in the cobbled streets of our northern cities.

Whatever the birth-pangs of such systems their relics are to be found wherever there are traces of that Roman civilisation whose other civil structures foreshadow those of the railway age. In Britain, for instance, rutted slabs are visible not only in museums but *in situ* at many of the forts along Hadrian's Wall, such as Housesteads. Crude pictograms in a language which was not to acquire its full vocabulary for nearly 1500 years, these grip the imagination with speculations as to just what it was which impeded the Romans from devising a true tramway system; and so it is perhaps surprising that no comprehensive survey appears to have been carried out on the gauges of Roman wagons. Such research, at least in the British Isles, appears an ideal project for the amateur archaeologist and might finally settle the 4 ft. 8½ in. *canard.*

Inclined planes may have appeared in Europe as early as the twelfth century; and certainly the massive building projects of late Norman and early Gothic times would have revived the conditions needed for the temporary (and perhaps accidentally-formed) guided way. From the fourteenth century onwards, too, the emergence of such industries as the casting of cannon must have led to inter-works or works-to-river transport systems a hundred yards or so in length, as well as to the still shorter conveyors used in the working of saw-mills, masons' yards, grain mills and the like. Scholars mistrust the use of such terms as 'must' and 'would have', since they presuppose precisely the type of phenomena on which conclusions should be founded. But when these phenomena are of their nature transient guesswork must be resorted to; and certainly little clear evidence of the use of these devices appears before the shattering but still-uncertain age of the mediaeval-to-renaissance transition.

From about 1530 onwards, though, they became increasingly common, those woodcuts showing industrious apprentices pushing tracked trolleys through foundry, mine, dockyard or powder mill. Some may have stemmed only from their artist's imagination and have been as thinly rooted in reality as were Leonardo's flying machines and sophisticated machine tools. But though no tangible relics could be expected to have survived, there is little doubt that both the guiding and the friction-reducing qualities of systems of parallel tracks were recognised in Britain (as in those other countries where the technological revolution was beginning to take shape) some four hundred and fifty years ago. In the damper countries they had another advantage: wagons did not become mud-logged in bad weather.

By now, too, the tramway proper—the system whose length is measured in hundreds of yards if not in miles—was in sight: such lines appear to be illustrated in Agricola as early as 1556 and even in Sebastian Munster's work published some years before. The location of the world's first such system may never be determined. But it was almost certainly in what may (in the very broadest sense of the phrase) be called central Europe—perhaps as far east as Hungary, perhaps as far west as Lorraine, or perhaps in the Harz.

The reason why Britain does not figure among these possibilities is that the tramways on the first phase of the technological revolution, like their successors, were essentially adjuncts to mines. Another century and a half were to pass before its second phase—and with it Britain's prosperity—was to be founded on deep-mined coal and on iron extracted on a scale much greater than that of a 'cottage' industry based on local concentrations of charcoal-producing forests and surface-dug ore. The armaments industry has always attracted heavy state investment and so led in numerous technical (and particularly metallurgical) developments, and so far as the casting of cannon and naval fittings was concerned the world was then still largely in the Bronze Age. Britain's few and ill-drained deep mines, producing mainly tin and lead, handled a tonnage tiny by comparison with that of the copper mines of the continent; and it was hence there that the tramway saw the light of day.

Many of the earliest examples, however, never did this in the literal sense, for they were subterranean systems. In common with modern works lines, too, they were dismantled and relaid as old galleries were worked out and new ones opened. More permanent were the inclines arranged to carry ore from mine-heads to the staithes of the rivers which were for centuries more to afford the world its main means for the long-distance haulage of heavy freight.

By definition, such rivers ran along valley-floors: the mine adits were typically in mountainous country well above them: and hence arose the need for cable-assisted ascents. (It is not clear, though, that the 'self-acting' principle by which the weight of descending laden wagons provided the motive power to draw up empties was used before a British patent of 1750 which also covered the 'cistern system' of water counter-balances. After this date it impressed several generations as an edifying example of human ingenuity trading-in on divine providence). But at one or both ends of the incline were often to be found more conventional systems in which wagons were man-handled or drawn by horse, mule, donkey or ox along timber rails.

Such was the typical continental tramway which may date back as far as the earlier years of the sixteenth century. It was destined for a remarkably long life—possibly even for a longer one than the present-day railway will achieve, for wooden rails were still being laid in the later 1800s. But though there are claims that the tramway, like the mining pump, was brought over by the German engineers imported fairly early in the reign of Elizabeth I there is no certain evidence that surface systems were known in Britain before 1600. This date is still three years before the queen's death and sixteen before Shakespeare's, as well as being more than 150 years earlier than any which the ordinarily well-informed person would associate with the tramway age.

A recent paper has established that a two-mile track was built by the owner of a large and technically advanced colliery at Wollaton, Nottinghamshire, in 1603 or 1604; and in default of well-documented rival claims this must be accorded its title of "England's First Rails." It is interesting that the tracks, though constructed only from timber frames laid on roughly-levelled ground, were at the time referred to as "rayles", the distinction between a railway and a tramway (and the latter term, rarely used before 1800, seems to derive from an old word for 'to draw' and certainly has little to do with Benjamin Outram) being one of retrospective convenience only. The visitor to Wollaton Lane today will find no trace in this heavily-built-up area of the 'new and extraordinary inventions and practises' of more than three hundred and fifty years ago, and all that can be surely said is that this is the oldest established railway site in Britain. But as such it merits a pilgrimage—and, one would have thought, some form of memorial plaque.

The proprietor of the Wollaton line was Huntington Beaumont. Beaumont—who has other claims to be remembered as an engineer—shortly afterwards acquired an interest in collieries in Northumberland, and built tramways there too. The fact that two other early mine-owners had a line running for about a mile to the Severn at Calcutts near Broseley (Salop) in 1605, however, suggests that Beaumont was no isolated fanatic but rather one of a number of men moving with a trend of the times.

The growth of colliery tramways thereafter was steady rather than spectacular, and the next recorded date is 1645 when a four-and-a-half mile line is claimed to have been begun south from Dunston in Co. Durham. But numerous others followed in the same county and across the Tyne in Northumberland (indeed, the invention which had originated in Nottingham now became known as a 'Newcastle road'), and before the end of the century South Wales had its first wagon-way—which was also linked to a very early canal at Melyn works near Neath, Glamorgan. The majority of these later seventeenth century tracks have been completely swallowed-up by subsequent relaying, mining or building, even their gauges usually being unknown. But the Ryton Moor line in Co. Durham, opened before the plague year of 1665, has left earthworks such as those at Crawcrook to survive for more than three centuries and to be claimed as not merely the oldest substantial artefacts of the tramway age in Britain but the only ones dating from the 1600s.

By 1676 the tramways of the north-east were becoming a source of wonderment to the curious traveller. The eighteenth century brought no immediate technical innovations; but it witnessed Britain's development from an imitator of continental mining practices into an initiator, and an acceleration in the pace of tramway building. Henceforth, then, we can mention only those lines of which some memorial subsists. And, by the most fortunate of fates, Britain's oldest remaining masonry work of the tramway age has not merely survived for nearly two hundred and fifty years virtually intact but is a genuinely impressive witness (it is one of the few railway relics scheduled as an Ancient and Historic Monument) to the skills of those half-forgotten civil engineers who practised at a time when even the pioneers of the canal age were unborn.

The Dunston line in Durham referred to above, which was extended to run south-west for some seven miles to collieries on Tanfield Moor, was rebuilt about 1725 as the sources of coal nearest to the ports were becoming exhausted and the search for supplies moved inland. (This is probably the first line to which a gauge—in this case 3 ft. 10 in.—can be ascribed.) Several earthworks as well as part of the trace can still be studied: for instance an embankment some hundred feet high and three hundred feet broad at the base remained in use for a mineral line until very recently. But these are eclipsed in interest by the impressive Causey arch constructed in 1727 by a local mason, Ralph Wood, who had also built a timber predecessor.

Though it was being viewed by aquatintists of the very early 1800s as a picturesque, Salvator-Rosa-like ruin and is today almost invisible for greenery, this single stone arch of quite sophisticated construction which spans over a hundred feet and rises more than sixty high still stands as a gate to the greater works of the railway age proper. It most certainly makes the point that the English transport engineers were now mastering their art and that for the next hundred and fifty years a British 'first' in this field was almost certainly a world first as well.

Parts of the neighbouring system of Derwenthaugh and the Pontop collieries date from as early as 1712, though the network was not completed until 1790: from this, earthworks survive in the strangely-mixed countryside near Byermoor—at Harelaw, for instance. In Northumberland, where

PLATE 1

Three facets of the railway past are united in this picture of the Brighton Belle near Merstham, Surrey. The stock dates back to the electrification of the line in the early 1930s: the track, with its graceful bridge, was built at the end of the nineteenth century to provide a relief for Rennie and Rastrick's original and parallel line of the late 1830s. and across the valley in the background ran the course of the Croydon, Merstham and Godstone tramway opened at the beginning of that century.

PLATE 2

Tramways in South Wales. Above is the trace of the Penydarren line—the scene of Trevithick's first experiments with locomotion—passing under a later GWR branch near Quaker's Yard, Glamorgan. Left and below are views of the scenic Brynoer tramway nearby.

PLATE 3

Early rolling-stock, as illustrated by (above) what is probably the world's oldest passenger rail vehicle, now preserved at Camborne, Cornwall, and (below) the last wagon to see service on the Stratford-upon-Avon tramway.

PLATE 4

Above, railway historians examine the cast iron bridge near Robertstown, Glamorgan, of 1811, which is almost certainly the world's oldest rail bridge of metal. The Haie Hill tunnel in the Forest of Dean, below, was opened in 1809 and remained in service after more than 160 years.

too a consortium of colliery-owners known as the Grand Allies were from 1726 onwards to prove a power on the tramway scene, the oldest works are probably those dating from about 1690 at Horton Bridge on the Plessey tramway serving Blyth harbour; but a more historic line was that which ran five miles west from Lemington to pits near Wylam on the Tyne. Opened in 1748 (and on a five foot gauge) by Mr. Blackett, this was of course to acquire fame at a later stage in transport development before being converted to a conventional mineral line.

In Cumberland the earthworks of the Parker Waggonway at Whitehaven, which dates from 1738 and was celebrated by the poetaster Weepes, can be seen at Monkwray Brow: this may be the earliest line of which at least the surname of the engineer can be cited. (It was Spedding.) And meanwhile a solitary but casually historic line had been built north of the Border, the two-and-a-half-mile Tranent–Cockenzie railway in East Lothian which was opened in 1722. From this not only does most of the trace survive but a handful of stone sleeper blocks dating from a relaying of 1815 can be seen at the entrance to the picturesque Old Harbour. The line itself is remarkable as having been the site of the first railway battlefield, since the cannon mounted by General Cope against the Jacobite rebellion stood along its length where it had more than two decades before crossed the field of Prestonpans.

Meanwhile, far from the incipient grime of the earliest centres of the industrial revolution, John Wood had in 1731 supervised the construction of the new town of Bath—and, in particular, the transport of massive quantities of freestone from quarries at Coombe Down to the shores of the Gloucestershire Avon. To aid this traffic a 3 ft. 9 in. tramway was built, probably on the model of a Hampton Down line constructed six years earlier.

The quarry owner was the wealthy postmaster, Ralph Allen; the engineers, John Padmore and Richard Jones, and the most characteristic feature of the system a detached inclined plane, built in 1755, which sliced through the grounds of Allen's Prior Park estate and down to the river near the Palladian Bridge. The trace—over a mile long, and with a maximum gradient of 1/10—is today used as a roadway. Quite apart from the unexpectedness of its situation on the outskirts of Britain's most elegant of cities, the Prior Park line is of note on two grounds: it is the first tramway connected with coal, and it also affords the earliest evidence of an incline in this country—though it was not of the cable-hauled, counter-balanced type. Considering that inclines imply major earthworks, this suggests that the device itself, despite its early origins in German Europe, was not employed in Britain on any substantial scale before the eighteenth century. One or two earlier lines, however, probably ended in short and moveable lengths of cable-worked track leading down to rivers and harbours.

Less than a dozen sites have been mentioned so far, but these include all those where it is agreed that traces of surface lines pre-dating 1750 are still to be found. The story, perhaps, should not be regarded as closed. But if there are additions to be made, these are more likely to be found in outworked areas than in the dense countrysides of the Tyne and Wear, where the typical fate of an early tramway was not to be abandoned in rural solitude but rather to be re-worked into a Victorian mineral line.

Furthermore, the amateur industrial archaeologist will not need reminding that from this period he can hope for no more discoveries than additions to the documentary evidence, a half mile of trace on the land, perhaps an embankment, just possibly the abutment of an overbridge. Permanent ways were in those days of wood and so exceedingly perishable: railway 'furniture' was almost unknown: and one would be fortunate indeed to unearth a hoard of flanged wheels cut from solid timber such as were discovered near Broseley at the turn of the century.

The year 1750, in which Britain's tramway systems probably totalled over a hundred miles, has been arbitrarily chosen to mark the conclusion of a prelude *to* a prelude: an overture is ending, but is itself giving way only to a curtain-raiser. No sovereign ascended in that year, no war began or ended: according to one dictionary of events, indeed, nothing whatever happened in it. It is simply a convenient mid-century point of rest.

But industrially things were far from restful. Britain's economy was becoming increasingly based on coal for extraction as well as for fuel, and not only the metallurgical but the ceramic industries were beginning to work in terms of tons rather than pounds. The cumulative effect of such trends as urbanisation, a great increase in population and hence agricultural activity, and a dependence on international trade, were already becoming apparant: the need for new sources of power was making itself acute: and above all the demand was for vastly improved arteries of transport.

The immediate development was to be the linking of Britain's harbours, coalfields, manufacturing centres and rivers—the last of which had been steadily improved for navigation since at least Elizabethan times—by a national network of canals. But water could not reach everywhere; and so the period from 1760 to 1830, which is commonly referred to as the canal age, was also the classic age of the tramways.

# II *TRAMWAYS, 1750-1800*

ONLY eight years after the mid-point of the eighteenth century, another of Britain's half-dozen classic precursors of the railway age began its long history. This was the six-mile Middleton railway system in south Leeds which, since its proprietor Charles Brandling built it under the first of parliamentary acts, may indeed be entitled to the much-debated appellation of 'the world's oldest railway'. In its original form, however, it was a pure tramway laid with wooden rails on a four-foot gauge to carry a traffic restricted to coal.

The destiny of early tramway routes resembles that of Roman roads in that some have vanished almost without trace, others sleep below grass in a more or less clearly recognisable state (and from the date which one has now reached onwards there is scope for real research by the amateur of industrial archaeology, particularly in view of the threats from motorways and housing estates), and others again have been overlaid by later, and perhaps still used, transport ways on the same general course. But even with these last some trace of the original works may often be unearthed metaphorically if not literally; and the Brandling railroad has had a history as fortunate as it is varied.

Most of this history—the conversion to Blenkinsop rack-working in 1812, the reversion to horse traction, the later rebuilding as a conventional mineral line, and then the closure of all except a brief length (though one including a substantial viaduct) which was incorporated into the main-line railways—lies outside the scope of this chapter. So too does the story of the recent, and most enterprising, revival of the central section of the system by an enthusiasts' society. But specimens of rack-rail remain in Leeds Museum and the BRB (York) collection, and even from Brandling's original line three memorials survive amid a tangle of later tracks and of pathways which mark abandoned ones.

The first is the general trace, which was followed in subsequent rebuildings—and even, at one period, by an urban electric tramway which duplicated the line for a mile or so as on the attractive but now-demetalled run though Middleton Park. (A crossing of rail and tram tracks, however, has survived). Most of the system is now enclosed by factory walls, but the line crosses public highways at Moor Road (Junction) and Burton Road. Secondly, Brandling's incline—now known as the 'Old Run', since it was by-passed by a later realignment—remains visible as a roadway with the 'Engine Inn' at its foot. And finally, at Hunslet Moor, some earthen banks incorporating old stone sleepers are recognisable as the platforms or staithes (a word adopted from waterway practice) at which coal was loaded.

Some of these works are in the situation—almost unique among railway antiquities—of being protected by the National Trust. But the ordinary enthusiast visiting Leeds may be pardoned for preferring to such relics—and even to the reminiscence that the Middleton was probably the first line to use a signal—the fact that he can watch daily commercial working on an alignment of which most is well over two hundred years old. By prior arrangement he may be able to travel over it too.

Some other tramways of this period which have survived in at least the sense of leaving partly-traceable routes are to be found at Whitefield south of the Tyne in Co. Durham (with earthworks at High Spen and Greenside dating from between 1660 and 1708), north of the Wear near Fatfield (a system originating before 1710 which later totalled nearly thirty miles and has left earthworks at Brackenbeds), and at Lambton on the opposite bank where a ten-mile system commenced in the 1770s has left a much later tunnel at Belmont Ridge. At Broughton Moor, Cumberland, the surviving White Gill embankment near Maryport dates from 1775, and near Kirkhouse below Tindale Fells in the same county not only several cuttings and embankments but a weigh-house at Brampton Sands remain from a colliery line commenced in 1775 whose later alignment is clearly visible. The weigh-house itself dates from 1799 and is hence possibly Britain's oldest railway building.

There are also two interesting routes of four or five miles linking the coalfields of Fife (Scotland) to the Forth. The Halbeath railway running inland from Inverkeithing was opened in 1780 and is now represented by a ruined bridge at Halbeath near Clarkston, and from St Davids to Fordell a 4 ft. 4 in. gauge line was built soon after 1769. Its short tunnel at Crossgates, however, probably dates from no earlier than 1833.

Documentary evidence exists of a number of other late-eighteenth-century tramways being built in the English midland counties. But of these history can write only 'no trace'. The main reason why independent lines of this date are rare south of a line drawn from the Mersey to the Tyne is that in all but the most mountainous country the canal now appeared the most economical means of bulk transport, and that the tramway inevitably became subsidiary to it. Since these canal lines present features of their own, it is perhaps best to defer considering them for a few pages and instead mention a still more important direction of development.

Up to now, tramways had remained of timber throughout, though there had been minor improvements such as the use of softwood rails with replaceable facings of hardwood. The typical tramway of the 1750 period, indeed, had become fairly sophisticated in construction: with its four-inch-square rails spiked down at close intervals to heavier, ballasted transverse sleepers it was closer in basic engineering to the lines of today than were many of the formative experiments of the railway age proper. But two developments were at hand, the use of stone (and usually granite) blocks about one foot cubically and weighing over a hundredweight in place of timber sleepers, and the change to iron running rails.

The former step, though of dubious technical value, was at least to benefit today's industrial archaeologists, for a march of stone blocks in the ground is unambiguous. (Samuel Smiles attributed this innovation to Outram about 1800, but earlier examples survive.) Concerning the latter, one should note that some early lines had used wrought-iron rail facings on hard-worked stretches even though the wheels which ran over them remained of wood. Similarly, iron tyres were occasionally used on wooden tracks from 1726 onwards, and cast-iron wheels followed soon after.

In the next stage of the story the action returns to the valley of the Severn at Coalbrookdale, Salop. Thanks to the use of coke for smelting by the Bristol Quaker, Abraham Darby, this had become the centre of iron-making during its transition from what was almost a branch of forestry into a modern production industry. And there on November 13, 1767—or over a decade before the historic iron bridge was assembled—a number of rails were cast for the experimental relaying of part of the local tramway system to Ketley. (Plate 5).

This had itself been opened in 1750 and involved an incline at Jiggers Bank which is still visible together with an embankment at Coalmoor. Including neighbouring colliery lines, the network (which operated on a wide variety of gauges) soon totalled nearly nineteen miles. Those who seek the atmosphere of these parts (where the old tramway routes are incorporated as footpaths in new housing schemes), rather than precise archaeological information, are referred to John Betjeman's fantasy on Captain Webb of channel swimming and matchbox fame.

The Coalbrookdale rails were themselves supported on wooden members and followed timber-way practice by being of the plain, rectangular type later known as 'bar' rails. They engaged with wooden wheels flanged on their inside faces or which, in a few cases, were of pulley form. Only a little later did the L-section 'plateway' appear: and the rivalry between these two, and other forms of track, was not to develop fully until the next century.

The present owners of the Coalbrookdale Iron Co.—that 'very responsible and opulent company', as an early historian put it—have established a private museum at Darby Road, Coalbrookdale. Open in summer, it houses a number of interesting exhibits—including one of the first importance—relating to early iron-founding. But it should be stressed that the plateway turnout and lower part of a wagon exhibited there date from a later relaying of the line and are not of the 1767 pattern, and that not all of the information publicised by the company is now considered accurate.

At Horsehay on the same system a length of plateway remains in place and was until very recently used for works purposes, and another section of Coalbrookdale track forms part of the substantial railway collection of the City Museum of Leicester. The smaller exhibits of this authority—it may be noted here—can be seen at Newarke House; the larger are either in store or displayed at the former Stoneygate tram depot.

In any case the Shropshire experiment proved an economical one, and some fifty miles of rail were cast at Coalbrookdale in the next few years. But even for new lines (which were now being built at such a rate that only those which have left substantial remains can be noted here) the adoption of iron was slow, and apart from a few examples in Derbyshire and perhaps Yorkshire they did not become popular until the late 1780s. Not until the end of the century—and particularly after the introduction of chaired track in Northumberland about 1797—was there a widespread conversion of wooden to iron tramways of any form.

Towards the end of the century, however, there was substantial tramway-building activity in the country of the Welsh marches: many of the tracks then laid were iron edgeways even though one or two followed earlier timber tracks, and these represent the earliest survivors of their type. Thus, of a row of four limestone lines which connected with the now-abandoned Montgomeryshire arm of the Shropshire Union canal between Crickheath and Llanymynech (Salop), each has left remains. Reading from north to south, these are earthworks at Llynclys; a curious bridge under the platforms of the later Pant station with another arch in the canal bridge there, and an incline on the hill above: three inclines at Pen-y-Foel near Llanymynech; and two bridges under Welshpool Road in that town.

Further south, another line of this period met the unfinished Leominster canal at the still standing Wharf House near Mamble, Salop. (Plate 6). And in the rather unexpected vicinity of Sandycroft, on the lower Dee in Flintshire, there was opened about 1801 a seven-mile plateway carrying bricks and coal. From this there have survived substantial earthworks at Newthorpe Farm, Ewloe, and Daniels Ash near Hawarden, the last being a particularly fine embankment for the times.

In Stirlingshire, Scotland, a two-mile line from the Kinnaird collieries to the Carron ironworks was laid as an iron-capped timber way in 1760, is believed to have been converted to an edge-rail system in 1795, and (since it operated as a mineral railway in the present century) is still traceable; and nearby in Clackmannan a most unusual short system was built between 1766 and 1771 by the Erskine of Mar, though probably with wooden rails which were not iron-capped until 1785 nor replaced by all-iron rails until a little later still. A branch of this ran alongside Castle Street, Alloa, with spurs entering a glassworks and a whisky distillery—thus considerably diversifying the coal and iron which were the staples of the line. Two otherwise inexplicable tunnels or bridges under the side-streets of Alloa, each about forty feet long, fortunately remain from this system.

Meanwhile the canal network which had begun about 1760 with lock-free lengths in the Mersey area was spreading across the heart of England in the general form of James Brindley's silver saltire. The moral that healthy profits could be won by organising transport on a national rather than a parochial basis was not lost on men of the calibre of Outram, who before 1800 was arguing that all future tramways should be built to a common form, gauge (Outram suggested 4 ft. 2 in.) and even ruling gradient to allow for interconnection. But this dream was not to be realised for another thirty years.

For the present the waterways were in the ascendancy, and the tramways had to follow their flag.

For the canals certainly did not put the tramroads out of business as the railways were later to outmode the waterways. For some fifty years the two transport media were to expand in comparative harmony, despite the Duke of Bridgewater's misgivings concerning 'those damned tramroads', with the canals forming the main lines and wooden or iron tramways acting as feeders to them or bridging gaps in difficult country. Only in a few cases were there disputes as to the better form, and very rarely was a tramway converted to a waterway or vice-versa. On the whole, canal construction (and the concomitant improvement of rivers and harbours) encouraged tramway construction in an age when roads remained so bad that there was a constant temptation to drive ordinary wagons along the tramroad beds and commerce continued to expand: the majority of new lines now were indeed owned by canal companies, and the same engineers worked in both media.

Nowhere was this truer than in South Wales and Monmouthshire, where the 'dram' roads may have received their present name. There over three hundred miles of coal-and-iron-based tramways were built around 1800; and eventually almost all were linked to canals, rivers or harbours. Traces of the past are, however, harder to identify than to discover in these labyrinthine valleys where industry lies like a palimpsest: early records are few, industrial archaeology has, perhaps, received less attention than in some other areas of Britain, and whilst the following list includes the more interesting certain survivors of eighteenth-century transport, the area which it covers can also show a large number of engineering works which *may* belong to the period. These include not only inclines (which, though visible everywhere in industrial Wales, are particularly difficult to date since their building is unlikely to have been recorded outside long-lost works' accounts), but impressive bridges over such rivers as the Glamorgan Tawe and Taff.

Of the 3 ft. 4 in. edge-rail systems built about 1795 to link with the Monmouthshire and Brecon and Abergavenny canals there remains a bridge over Prince Street, Blaenavon, earthworks and stone sleeper blocks at Victoria Road, Pontymoile, and (a rare survivor, if it is indeed still *in situ*) a mile-post at Aberyschan. Glamorgan has stone sleepers at Cefn Coed-y-Cymmer and a bridge at Cyfarthfa (both of 1792) associated with the Glamorganshire or Cardiff canal, and other sleepers and a substantial causeway at Hirwaun from a 1794 edgeway; both these brief lines were mainly dependent on the carriage of limestone. In Brecknockshire, the extended canal (uniquely amongst those of South Wales) remains navigable, so that from a waterborne base one can study the remains of the so-called Brecknock and Abergavenny railway—an eight-mile system, opened in 1795 as an edge tramway but converted to a plateway, whose main commodity was pig-iron—at Gilwern (an underbridge to the canal), Beaufort and Nantyglo (earthworks) and Brynmawr (another bridge). In the same county the Abercrave incline of a short limestone line of 1798 to the Swansea canal is identifiable.

In England, the relics of late-eighteenth-century tramways which functioned as subsidiaries of waterway or harbour companies include the Gathurst incline of what was certainly misnamed 'Hustlers railway', which was opened before 1776 at the Lancashire end of the Leeds and Liverpool canal. Across the Pennines the same canal connected, at the end of its intriguing 'Springs' branch at Skipton, Yorks, with quarries at Haw Bank Rock: in its mile of running this line of 1786 or earlier involved a cutting and bridges at Bailey Cottage which can still be discovered amid the Earl of Thanet's woods. Also in Yorkshire, but linked to the Calder and Hebble navigation, is a viaduct at Flockton from the three-mile colliery tramway to Horbury Bridge which was opened about 1773 with wooden rails and subsequently converted: like several such systems, this has left enough marks on the ground to be envisageable throughout even when only doubtfully traceable. This last phrase applies also to the course of the brief Greasbrough tramway which from before 1763 ran west from Cinder Bridge on the Don, first as a timber and then as a plateway.

Another Pennine county, Derbyshire, was more extensively penetrated at this period by canals and their associated tramroads. The most spectacular example was not to be realised until after the Napoleonic wars; but as early as 1796 the still-navigable Peak Forest canal had been prolonged from its terminus at Bugsworth for seven miles south-east to limestone and gritstone quarries. Bugsworth has now, in deference to local susceptibilities, renamed itself Buxworth; but at least the upper section of Outram's spectacular 4 ft. 2 in. plateway (which was probably the first to adopt twenty-four-hour working, and which was not finally abandoned until 1922) can be rollowed. In addition to a mile run of stone sleeper-blocks, its features include the built-over trace of a self-acting incline near Chapel-en-le-Frith with stables at the top and part of an eighty-five-yard tunnel at Chapel Milton which may be England's oldest. A more definite claim is that a wagon used on the Peak Forest line, and built in the year after its opening, is the oldest complete rail vehicle surviving. This is preserved by the BRB in its York museum: some contemporary stock is privately held, and intriguing fragments can even be found scattered along the route.

On the eastern or Derwent side of the Peak watershed the presence of William Jessop's (still partly-watered) Cromford canal led to the building in 1793 of a small limestone-carrying system at Crich: its owners were the Butterley Company which had been founded three years before (with Jessop and Outram as early partners) and which thereby began an association with Britain's railways which has now lasted for more than 175 years. The lines were frequently relaid and not abandoned until 1930; and it is pleasant to note that the uppermost half-mile of the system now houses the working museum of urban trams referred to in a later chapter of this book. Traces of two inclines which descend from its southern end are also clear, and bridges survive at Fritchley.

On the southern or Trent side of the Derbyshire massif, a 3 ft. 6 in. plateway was built by Outram in 1795 over the four miles from the Derby canal's basin at Little Eaton north to Smithy Houses. Carrying stone, pottery and other products as well as coal, this 'gang road' too was to be long-lived, being little changed by 1908. It has also left notable remains—a bridge (called Jack o'Darley's: the parapet is later) at one end, a culvert at the other, and earthworks between. A section of the track, mounted on stone blocks, is preserved by the National Coal Board at the now-closed Drury Lowe colliery near Smithy Houses.

In Leicestershire, the route of Jessop's two-mile Thringstone system linking collieries to what is now the Grand Union canal can be traced: it dates from 1796. In Staffordshire a branch of the Trent and Mersey canal connected with some lines of eventful history, probably dating from 1777, at Froghall basin. This limestone system—the Caldon Low—was opened with wooden rails about 1777, changed to iron bars, was realigned as a plateway by John Rennie in 1802, and after further rebuilding as a cable-operated line did not close until 1920. It has bequeathed bridges at Woodcock (ruined) and Whiston (intact), an embankment at the latter, the traces of three self-acting inclines at Whiston, Upper Cotton and Froghall and a cutting near the eastern terminal—now spelt Caldenlow—at Hoften's Cross, as well as a traceable route. The neighbouring Consall line from the river Churnet to Weston Coyney, a seven-mile plateway of 3 ft. 6 in. gauge laid on stone sleepers, may date from the same period: amongst other remains this has left a bridge under the A522 road at the curiously-named Tunnel Farm south of Wetley Rocks.

This selection of tramways of the later eighteenth century has been artificial in that its criterion has been the accidental one of the survival of an authenticated line despite the hazards of that element which still antiquates antiquities. Many other examples, such as the Golden Valley lines of Derbyshire, *may* have left traces which belong to this period; and in such cases the amateur archaeologist can render a real service in pursuing dates and allocating priorities. Furthermore, from about 1770 onwards there is increasing scope for new discoveries of the type made on the ground rather than through libraries.

But details should not be allowed to obscure the cardinal fact that the later eighteenth century was marked by not only an expansion of the national tramway system to some five hundred miles (including individual systems of over thirty miles) but by a high degree of cross-fertilisation in industry as a whole. As a result of this, for instance, a company engaged in laying down early iron tramways was probably at the same time casting cylinders and rolling boiler plates for Newcomen engines and fabricating canal aqueducts too. Ruling all these developments was the final consummation of the trend from natural materials and copper alloys towards cast and wrought iron as the basis for engineering.

By 1800 the timber tramway was beginning to pass from the scene, to be succeeded by the age which Bertram Baxter defined as that of 'stone blocks and iron rails', and wood was thenceforth used only on the briefest works lines. The minority of tramways not relaid with more durable materials would soon have been cannibalised to feed the domestic grates of seven generations ago, and hence there is little enough chance that a wooden sleeper—let alone running rail—remains undiscovered on the surface of Britain. But recently a discovery came the way of a Glasgow steel company which was not only in itself an example of archaeological serendipity, but which suggests that one cannot rule out the possibility that hidden tracks dating back even to Elizabethan times remain to be discovered.

This company had inherited a lead mine at Groverake, Co. Durham, which itself probably dated back to the fifteenth century but had been abandoned in 1908. The shafts were, however, littered with fluorspar then discarded as spoil but now regarded as a valuable steelmaking flux. It was while removing some of this from a waterlogged drift in 1957 that there came to light no less than 150 yards of 1 ft. 9 in. track made of local black oak and mounted on sleepers of the same timber, the whole system being much decayed but quite unmistakeable.

The level in which it was found was known to have been opened in 1816—at which time, by a pleasant coincidence, the mine was owned by a descendant of the Huntington Beaumont who had been the first to introduce tramways to Britain. The track itself may well have been transferred from a shallower, outworked lode. But it is clear that timber had not yet reached the end of its history as a material for rails: indeed, another working dating from 1850 yielded a set of points of wood plated with iron, and wooden rails dating from the later nineteenth century have also been found in Derbyshire lead mines and elsewhere.

So the oldest survivor of Britain's wooden tramways was found in a similar situation to that in which the first was probably laid, a place hidden from the sun. A section of the Groverake metals is now preserved in the railway museum, York. One may be tempted to agree with Baxter's stricture that so small an example forms 'at best, a very unconvincing exhibit'; but it represents a transport medium which served Britain's expanding industries for more than 250 years, and which for the first 150 of those was virtually without a rival.

## *III TRAMWAYS, 1800-1830*

THROUGHOUT the 1700s the standard of civil engineering on the best tramways had so improved that in this respect Stephenson would have had little to teach Outram. But even more important than the technical developments of the age was the fact that the tramways had ceased to be purely an inter-works convenience and had (at least as a handmaiden to the canals) begun to play a part in a national transport network. As the nineteenth century opened in Britain—where it was to prove the most dynamic period which the world has ever known and probably ever will—there were an increasing number who foresaw the country being knit by a fabric of iron ways, possibly powered by steam. But those were still only a few, and in any case such political dreams were in advance of technical potentialities.

One important new concept, however, was translated to reality. This was that of the common carrier line which (like the canals themselves) should not be either formally or in practice tied to one or two works but should accept all local traffic. This was not to be the dominant theme of the pre-Napoleonic—or even pre-Victorian—beginning of the century, which was perhaps not yet ready to cope with the land-acquisition problems involved: indeed, more than three decades were to pass before it began to prove its full value. But, fittingly enough, the world's first public railway in the above sense was opened in Britain over the first few years of the century.

Originally conceived as an adjuct to one of London's few waterway systems, but not itself canal-owned, the significantly-named Surrey Iron railway was built over the eight miles south from Wandsworth (via Mitcham, where there was a short branch to Carshalton) to Croydon between 1801 and 1803. From this section the only identifiable relic appears to be a pathway running from Summerstown Road, Wimbledon, to Colliers Wood, past Lambeth cemetary. But almost immediately William Jessop, the line's engineer, was asked to continue the track for a similar distance to Merstham and Godstone (Plate 1). The immediate targets were the quarries of this nearest flank of the downs, since limestone was in increasing demand to feed iron-making furnaces as well as for building purposes. But beyond that the line's proprietors dreamed of reaching Portsmouth, and even though the port eventually proved well out of their range the full distance was surveyed by Jessop as early as 1802.

A surprising number of remains subsists from the Godstone extension (which in fact itself probably terminated at Betchworth), though some are now threatened by roadworks. Thus, there is an embankment beside Chipstead Valley Road and a major cutting flanking the A23 at Harps Wood. The remains of two bridges can be seen at Dean Lane, Merstham, and two buildings associated with the system also survive nearby—Weighbridge Cottage (a typical example of a facility which had to be provided by every line accepting freight and loaded wagons from independent users), and Fox Shaw, formerly an inn. The route is traceable in several places, notably Avon Path, South Croydon; the BRB collection includes a single rail, and three sections of track have been re-erected—one on its original site in what is now Purley Rotary Field (Plate 5), another slightly off the route at the *Jolliffe Arms* (which is named after one of the contractors, the other being Edward Banks of London Bridge fame), and a third outside the branch library at Wallington. The recent excavation of one of these settled the long-debated question of the line's precise construction: the CMG (and almost certainly the SIR too) was a plain 4 ft. 2 in. plateway using stone sleeper blocks.

The Surrey system had powers to carry all forms of freight, and attracted international interest. As yet, however, neither *entrepreneurs* nor governments had realised that the immense revolution brought about by the coming of an economy based on coal and iron—if not yet on steam—had had its demographic effects, that a man's place of work was no longer synonymous with his residence, and that there was hence a need for passenger transport too. Almost accidentally, it seems (for this was an age of successful empiricism), such power were acquired by the next of Britain's pioneering lines, the Oystermouth railway.

Running from Brewery Bank near Swansea harbour for more than seven miles west across the Mumbles peninsula, this was opened in 1806 as a plateway (probably with double-flanged or trough-like rails) and began to carry passengers regularly in the next year. In the following century and a half it passed through almost every transmogrification possible, moving on from an edge-line to a steam tramway and then an electric interruban line. It is a cause for national regret that the local authorities were in 1960 allowed to abandon and totally efface this historic line to make way for traffic jams.

These precursors of the railway age were significant; but they were not typical, In the first decade of the nineteenth (as of the twentieth) century, transport activities generally continued in their existing directions of development. And at the time this implied an extension of the nation's canal network.

So profitable were waterways now proving that the owners of new canals were often unwilling to wait for the completion of long tunnels and lock flights before they began to draw revenue. These gaps were hence bridged by yet another—and designedly temporary—type of tramway. An early example was that which Outram built in 1800 for more than three miles above the Blisworth (Northants) tunnel on what is now the Grand Union canal. Five years later this had served its purpose and was reduced to a tow-path link; but it was substantially engineered as a double-track line and can still be traced as a footpath.

Much longer lived was the four-and-a-half mile plateway, known as the Preston and Walton Summit railway, which connected the Lancaster canal proper to what is now a branch of the Leeds and Liverpool canal; for this was opened in 1803 and, since the two sections were never joined by locks, remained in use until 1864. Its remains are considerable, comprising a short tunnel under Fishergate, Preston, and the remains of a bridge in Fordon Street, inclines at Averham and Penwortham which are among the first to have been worked by stationary steam engines, and several other earthworks including one embankment a half mile long. There is also an interesting wooden trestle bridge over the Ribble which, though not the first structure, is again among the oldest of its type surviving: and Robert Aickman compares Walton Summit itself to a lost city of the Incas.

Yet another example of a 'bridging' tramway was that which extended for about one and a half miles and was used between 1800 and 1807 to anticipate the opening of Marple (Cheshire) locks on the High Peak Canal. Limestone was off-loaded at the higher level and lime reloaded at the foot, the flow through the kilns hence being gravity-assisted. Another modern feature of this traffic is that iron tram/canal containers were used for easy transshipment. As with the contemporary Devizes line in Wiltshire the trace has now vanished amid overgrown side-pounds, but the kiln-house itself is still used as a private residence.

Tramways also played a part in maintaining service when canal sections gave persistent trouble; and a final type of such partnership is afforded by the several forms of barge-carrying incline which were experimented with thoughout the canal age. Curious—and in some cases important—as they were, though, these amphibious enterprises remain on the margins of early nineteenth-century land transport engineering. And despite some improvements in road-building in the south, this was primarily directed towards the expansion of conventional 'feeder' tramways.

In Lancashire, for example, a cluster of colliery lines (probably all four-foot edge-ways) were built or extended in the Wigan and St Helens area. Those with routes still partly traceable in this much-rebuilt zone included the Orrell railway at Crooke (an early user of rack locomotives) and the Altham and Read Hall of 1828. In Yorkshire, the Knottingley and Goole canal section was linked at Heck Bridge to the eight-mile Heck and Wentbridge edge railway, a limestone line opened about 1827 which has left earthworks at Little Smeaton and a bridge at Kirk Smeaton.

Further south the now-disused Dearne and Dove canal connected at Worsborough Bridge with a five-mile system of colliery tramways, originally built on a 4 ft. 3 in. gauge, which was begun in 1820 and survived for a full century: amongst other works this has left a bridge at Worsborough, earthworks at Rockley and a thirty-yard tunnel nearby at Broom Royd. And in the same area the Barnsley canal arm was extended from Barnby Bridge by a somewhat similar network (though one which also carried stone) laid between 1800 and 1830. This has left a long line of sleeper blocks—which are uniquely set in a close, diagonal formation—between Pot House and Silkstone church, a tunnel at Black Horse farm, and some embankments. Rails from the traceable Silkstone branch are preserved at York and in a private museum at Cawthorne (Yorks).

On the Cheshire/Stafford border, an embankment and stone sleepers survive at Kennel House of a line opened before 1817 to carry coal and stone from the Trubshaw area near the Trent and Mersey canal (Hall Green branch). In the same region the older but short-lived Congleton railway, whose track consisted of oval-section iron bars, has also left earthworks, whilst a section of plateway from the Longton and Fenton line—itself vanished—can be seen at the museum of Stoke-on-Trent. In Derbyshire, the Chesterfield canal was linked at Norbriggs Wharf to a brief colliery line of 1817 (earthworks at Norbriggs Farm near Renishaw), the Cromford canal at Hartshay near Pentrich to one of similar date (earthworks at Broadoak), and the Pinxton branch of the same waterway at Pinxton—where the stone sleepers still march across a field near Saff Lane—to a quite extensive system. The main line of this last, also engineered by William Jessop, was the eight-mile Mansfield and Pinxton railway which was opened to passengers in 1832 and later relaid: it has left earthworks at Grives Wood and Kings Mill (and from a subsidiary line at Berristow Farm), a bridge at Kirkby Mill, and specimens of the specially-designed edge-rails in Mansfield (Notts) museum and the BRB collection.

At Codnor Park Wharf the same canal met the Butterley Ironworks railway, which was also probably of this period and has left a bridge at Prospect Houses; and in Derbyshire too the Nutbrook or Shipley canal had a colliery line at West Hallam (with earthworks surviving at Northend Farm) dating from 1817. This county also preserves a number of other traceable lines which may belong to this period, so again there is scope for research.

Nottinghamshire has a bridge dating from 1817 at Brinsley Gin near a wharf on the Cromford canal; and at Willesley Basin on the partly-navigable Ashby-de-la-Zouch canal in Leicestershire there began a 4 ft. 2 in. plateway system, engineered by Outram, which ran to Cloud Hill and Ticknall in Derbyshire, totalled some fifteen miles, and carried mainly limestone and lime. The relics of this important line—which was originally built between 1802 and 1836, whose last right-of-way (maintained by one annual horse) was not abandoned until World War I, and which remains traceable for much of its course—are extensive: they comprise earthworks at Willesley Park, bridges at The Callis (Ashby: the parapet of this has been rebuilt), Heath End and Ticknall, and two notable tunnels near the last-mentioned village. One of these is 138 yards long; but the line also boasted the quarter-mile Old Parks tunnel which similarly survives, though not in its original form. In general Ashby and its environs form a half-forgotten area for those in search of traces of the industry as well as the leisure of the age loosely termed 'Regency'. Those who wish to study the line in more metropolitan surroundings will find a section of its track preserved at Leicester, and another is reported to be in place at Ashby Station.

The central midlands built comparatively few tramways at this period, preferring to extend their canals directly; but in England's mid-west several interesting lines have left traces. Gloucestershire west of the Severn should perhaps be treated together with South Wales. But on the 'English' side of the county two interesting systems were constructed.

Of the substantial Gloucester and Cheltenham railway there remain only scant traces; but this continued to Leckhampton as a quarry line which was in fact opened a year before its 'parent' in 1810 and operated for well over a century. Like the main line this was a 3 ft. 6 in. plateway, and it has left a number of inclines on Leckhampton Hill (with a winding-house to the lowest one) even though the traces in Cheltenham itself regrettably appear to have been destroyed.

The other line in the county, the ten-mile Bristol and Gloucestershire (or Coalpit Heath), belongs slightly outside the period of this chapter since it was opened in 1832 as a 4 ft. 8 in. edgeway. It was also linked to the river Avon rather than the Berkeley canal. Here too the original main and general-traffic line has left no traces, even a mile-long tunnel, having been obliterated. But again a neighbouring line, the Avon and Gloucestershire colliery railway of the same year, has had better fortune.

Survivors here include bridges at Mangotsfield and Warmley, substantial earthworks across Siston Common, and short tunnels at Oldland Common and Willsbridge, the latter (now used to carry a water main) being accompanied by what Baxter describes as 'a remarkable rock cutting and stone embankment'. At Avon wharf below Keynsham the original weigh-house and other buildings can still be seen; and in a garden outside Stroud a local enthusiast has reconstructed lengths of track from this and a number of other early lines. These show the Avon and Gloucestershire to have used the 'fish-bellied' type of rail, stiffened between its points of support, which was experimented with in many forms throughout the first three decades of the last century. Other sections of this are held by the BRB and the Bristol museum, having been rescued from the task of supporting notice-boards on a derelict canal.

The Radstock railway in Somerset provides an unusual example of a canal being later—in this case, in 1815—converted into a plateway. (As an example of the bilateral relationship obtaining at this time, it is worth mentioning that the five-mile Gayton to Northampton tramway, whose rails had earlier seen service on the Blisworth tunnel line, was in the same year rebuilt as a steeply-locked canal arm). This plateway, which a section of track recently excavated near Radstock and preserved by the BRB suggests to have been of 3 ft. 6 in. gauge, ran for nearly nine miles from Midford on the Somerset coal canal and has left a 200-yard tunnel at Wellow, earthworks at Old Welton, Radstock, Single Hill and elsewhere, and sleeper blocks at Old Welton. Lengths of it were later incorporated into the Somerset and Dorset railway.

To complete the present list for the west country there is the unique case of the Haytor Granite tramway, which ran for ten miles from Ventiford Wharf at Teigngrace on the Stover canal in Devonshire to the Haytor quarries. Here not only the traffic but the 'rails' themselves were of the local stone from which several of London's monuments were built, these rails consisting of granite blocks of about 12 ft. × 9 in. × 6 in., laid lengthwise and grooved to a 4 ft. 3 in. gauge. The line was opened in 1820; and not only is much of its trace still clear across the moor but the granite slabs themselves (which were fashioned into primitive points, of which a specimen also survives) run uninterrupted for hundreds of yards. That this is so is, of course, thanks not only to the wildness of the country but also to the durability of the combined roadbed, sleepers and running rails and their unfitness for any other use.

One or two lines have intruded into the above survey which were linked, in the early fashion, to river rather than canal banks. In the north-east of England, however, natural waterways remained (as they still do) an important feature in transport, and the typical line from colliery to staithe hence continued to be built. In Northumberland, for instance, the route of the four-and-a-half mile Netherton system of 1819 can still be traced beside the Blyth river; while on the north bank of the Tyne were the Seaton Burn waggonway—ten miles of 3 ft. 6 in. track, later known as the Brunton and Shields line, which dates from 1826—the Battle Hill at Willington Quay of 1820 (with an embankment at Wallsend Burn and other traces of the route), the Killingworth West Moor 4 ft. 8 in. edgeway (which was opened in 1806 and has left earthworks at Forest Hall as well as the justly-preserved lineside cottage of the eminent George Stephenson), the neighbouring Killingworth New of 1830—with route only surviving—the short-lived Fawdon line at Scotswood of 1818 (again with a route which has at least in part survived), and the 1808 Kenton and Coxlodge near Wallsend.

This last—another edgeway aiming at a 4 ft. 8 in. gauge—was relaid in 1813 with Blenkinsop rack rails: its major features, including several inclines, have been built over, but the five-mile route is generally traceable. A final local curiosity is "Kitty's Drift", a three-mile drain from the East Kenton collieries to Scotswood which served as a waggonway in the first decade of the century.

South of the Wear in Co. Durham the eight-mile Londonderry system, named after a lordly owner, was extended in the Pittington area before 1827: it has left fairly extensive traces, including those of inclines at Benridge Bank, Stables and Chilton Moor. The Earl of Durham's railway (or, more humbly, Lambton or Newbottle waggonway) was begun in 1813 and has left an embankment at Grindon Lane and a bridge near Bishopswearmouth cemetery; and nearer Sunderland was the Hetton colliery railway. A 4 ft. 8 in. edgeway opened in 1822 and relying largely on cable traction, this latter has bequeathed inclines—both powered and self-acting—at Warden Law, and is of interest as being George Stephenson's first independent work of engineering. The shadow of this giant indeed dominates the age and countryside, though his next classic task must be left to another chapter.

Also in this northern group was a Yorkshire line linked to the Calder and Hebble navigation at Dewsbury, the White Lee (or Dewsbury and Birstall) railway of 1805 which has left some sleeper blocks just recognisable as

PLATE 5

Above: a typical mid-eighteenth century bridge at Ketley, Salop. Below: the only *in situ* survivor of the plates of the CMG line.

PLATE 6

Tramway/waterway interchanges in the country of the Welsh marches. Above, enthusiasts follow the old tracks to Wharf House, Mamble, Salop, where these met the unfinished Leominster canal. Below, the second arch of the bridge betrays the approach of another tramway dating from the close of the eighteenth century, in this case one feeding the Llangollen canal near Trevor.

PLATE 7

Close together in time are (above) the splendid bridge over the Warwickshire Avon of the Stratford tramway—one of the last of its kind—and (below) the winding-house at Bagworth on the Leicester & Swannington Railway. The gravity-assisted incline fell away behind the standing figure.

PLATE 8

The first bridge of the railway age is perhaps Bonomi's Skerne arch at Darlington (above) which still carries traffic. But the stone blocks of the Brusselton incline on the same system (left) remind one that in 1825 the tramway age was not yet over.

forming a parapet to a wall beside Staincliffe Road, Dewsbury. And at the far end of England one last example of the period must be mentioned, the Plymouth and Dartmoor railway which ran for nearly 26 miles (by a 'circuitous course', as Dendy Marshall politely puts it) from near the Mayflower Steps at Plymouth, Devon, through Yelverton, to granite quarries near Princetown.

This was opened in 1823 on a 4 ft. 6 in. gauge and used (amongst other types of permanent way, including granite blocks) the fish-bellied type of track known as Losh rails: a specimen of the latter is preserved by the BRB. Though its trace is not as continuously visible as that of the Haytor line, a short later branch has almost vanished, and the northern section was rebuilt as a conventional railway, much has also survived *in situ*. Notable are the 620-yard tunnel at Leigham (now threatened by building developments), the remains of a bridge at Peak Hill Lane, and earthworks at Little Down, Roborough Down and Colville Wood.

In the west of England, however, transport works in the Napoleonic period were largely linked to improvements of yet another type, those made for commercial or military reasons to ports and harbours. The north had its share of this type of tramway too, amongst those which have left traces there being the eight-mile Rainton and Seaham (Co. Durham) railway of 1828 with its embankment at Warden Law, its incline at Seaham harbour and its short tunnel at Copt Hill near Hetton-le-Hole. But the most interesting such remains are undoubtedly to be found in the south-west.

Near Poole Harbour, Dorset, for instance, the Middlebere plateway of 1806, which handled the specialised commodity of ball (or pipe-) clay, has left bridges under Wareham Road, Corfe, as well as earthworks; its three-mile track between Middlebere and Norden heaths provides an unusual walk. On the Isle of Portland in the same county a 4 ft. 9 in. stone-carrying edgeway was opened in 1826 and not abandoned until 1939, the sleeper blocks at Tout Quarries near Fortuneswell being still in place. And in Cornwall the Redruth and Chasewater (*sic*) left Point Quay, Devoran (also in 1826) to make a ten-mile course by way of Hale Mills and Pennance to Redruth: a four-foot edgeway, this carried a variety of mineral traffic and may also have experimented with passengers.

Earthworks and stone sleeper-blocks from this line are to be found all along its route—for instance, at Nantgiles—and a visit to it could be combined with one to the Holman museum at Camborne. (Plate 3). This preserves what is probably the world's oldest passenger carriage, a wagon from the five-mile Poldice ore-carrying plateway of about 1810 (from which too some sleepers still remain) which ran from Portreath harbour through Scorrier. The wagon has been fitted with seats and coachman's 'box', and is believed to have been a directors saloon.

Scottish relics of this period are fewer, but they include examples of river-, sea- and canal-linked lines. Thus, near Troon harbour in Ayr there are two bridges—one at Drybridge and the other the parapeted Fairlie bridge over the river Irvine whose four stone arches are each of forty feet span—surviving from the four-foot Kilmarnock and Troon plateway of 1811. This,

Scotland's first public railway (which, like England's first, was engineered by William Jessop) seems almost from its opening to have carried passengers as well as coal legally and regularly. Its main line, later augmented by a now-vanished edgeway branch, was nearly ten miles long and eventually used as a conventional railway.

In the same county Telford's equally-vanished Glasgow, Paisley and Ardrossan canal failed to reach the latter port and hence to connect with the Ardrossan and Johnstone railway—which itself was misnamed in that it reached only to Kilwinning, some five miles north. Opened (again by a small extension of the time-bracket of this chapter) in 1831, this was a 4 ft. 6 in. edgeway carrying sandstone as well as coal. Its relics include the remains of a bridge which slanted over the river Garnock at Dirrans Mill on one of its quite lengthy branches and whose piers now stand like lonely menhirs, and another bridge intact over the Lugton Water at Fergushill. In Clackmannanshire some traces are to be found of a five-mile colliery line opened before 1806 from Clackmannan pier to Devonside.

In Fife the Elgin railway, a well-engineered 4 ft. 3 in. edgeway, ran from the harbour of Charlestown (where Lord Elgin's stables may remain in use as a shop) for six miles north past Dunfermline: its history dates back to 1771, but the traces of two self-acting inclines near a town even then more celebrated for its black coal than its blood-red wine are of 1821. And finally, in the same county, the Newbigging line was opened about 1817 to bring limestone down to a harbour. Short though this was, it is the only representative of a whole system and has left not only the Starleyburn incline near Burntisland but the rumour of a mysterious-looking tunnel—which, being some 500 yards long, represented nearly half the length of the system—to vanish towards an underground quarry.

The most typical countryside of the water-linked tramways built between 1800 and 1830, however, was the valleys of South Wales: indeed, for present purposes not only Monmouthshire but the western marches of England must be grouped with these. The following list continues that given in the last chapter in selecting those out of a complex which have left tangible traces: many of them were in fact physically joined to earlier tramways.

In Brecknock the Hay railway was an international line, for the twenty-four-mile course of this 3 ft. 6 in. plateway which handled coal, lime and general traffic extended from Watton Wharf near the head of the Brecon canal to Eardisley in Herefordshire. It was opened about 1817, and its remains include a rebored 675-yard tunnel near Tal-y-Lyn which was in use until recently, embankments at Arrah Lodge and more impressively at The Warren, Hay, and bridges over the Afon Llynfi and the river Enig. Another, at Hay station, was eventually inherited by BR/WR as its Bridge No 60.

Linked to the Usk river was a similar plateway, the Brynoer tramroad from south of Talybont. Opened in 1815, this wound up the Collwn valley on a superb contour-following bench round the Black Mountains to Trevil and was independently continued south to the ironworks of Rhymney twelve miles away: it carried pit-props as well as minerals. Part of the Rhymney section is still busily worked as a limestone line by the former Richard

Thomas & Baldwins steelworks. The earthworks at Bryn Cefnog, Blaen Duffryn and elsewhere on the abandoned stretch are perhaps of less interest than the spectacular—and not over-strenuous—mountain walk afforded by the cornice-route itself. (Plate 2).

A shorter line opened about the same time was the plateway from Llangattock near Crickhowell (again on the canal) to the limestone caves of Daren, and later to Nantyglo: this has left an incline at Wern Watkin and stone blocks at the quarries and Brynglas, as well as a traceable route. Also in Brecknock, but linked to the Swansea canal, were the Palleg (or Cwm Tyrch) tramroad near Ynys-Cedwyn (1807: route traceable) and the later (1834) Claypons line from the same wharf. This climbed Drum Mountain (leaving as a feature an incline near the Coedcae farms) and after four miles reached Orllwyn, where it connected with an 'independent' system (in the sense of one not subsidiary to an inland navigation or port authority), the Brecon Forest tramroad or Christie's railway. Opened about 1825 as another 3 ft. 6 in. plateway carrying coal, timber and limestone, the latter has left a few earthworks along its largely traceable thirteen-mile route south from Devynock.

The Glamorgan part of the same Swansea canal connected at Pontardawe with the brief Allt-Wen system of 4 ft. 6 in. colliery plateways (1801: route traceable); but Glamorgan had several other important waterways. The Neath canal, for example, was extended from its terminal at Glyn Neath to Hirwaun by the Cefn Rhigos line, a 4 ft. 2 in. plateway of 1805 with a wide spread of traffic (but a short life) which has left the remains of a powered incline at Pont Walby. There it connected with Dr Bevan's railway which continued from 1807 onwards (and originally on the same gauge) to the Dinas stone quarries: this route too can be followed. Another traceable connection which probably belongs to this period was the Pontneddfechan 2 ft. 6 in. edgeway, which made a junction at Glyn Neath, carried silica moulding sand, and has left sleeper blocks at Pontneddfechan.

The Cwm Derlwyn line opened in 1800 left the canal at Maes-y-Marchog for a nearby colliery at Derlwyn Wood: again the route is still visible. The brief Resolven tramway falls well outside the chronological limit of this chapter, not being opened until 1837, but may be mentioned here since its remains consist of the centrally-pierced stone sleeper blocks whose use had generally died out before the Victorian era. And a final member of this group was known as 'Parson's Folly'. From Pant-y-Coed, it ran for six devious miles to the Blaen-Cregan collieries near Glyncorrwg, using a 3 ft. 3 in. gauge and an inverted-T edgeway. Though it most probably belongs to the present time-bracket its date is unattested; but much remains including an incline at Wenallt farm, two near Cefn Morfudd and two at Mynydd Forch Dwn, and the remains of bridges over the Pelenna at Tonmawr.

Still in the same county, the Glamorganshire or Cardiff canal was linked to the Castle Morlais line of 1803 which ran briefly north from a junction with the older and important—but vanished—Dowlais line at Penydarren, now a suburb of Merthyr Tydfil. Opened in 1803 as a plateway built from the start on mixed gauges of 4 ft. 2 in. and 2 ft. 9 in., this has left a traceable route with earthworks and sleeper blocks at Gwaun Farren. The Penydarren plateway proper, however, (Plate 2) left the canal at Abercynon and followed its banks northwards for nearly ten miles to the iron works whose products it carried. Opened in 1802—two years before Trevithick's use of steam traction—this historic 4 ft. 2 in. line has left two splendid (and almost identical) semi-elliptical bridges of 63 ft. span over the river Taff at Edwardsville and Greenfield, these being built in 1815 after one of their timber predecessors had collapsed under load: there are also sleeper blocks at Merthyr Vale and Pontygwaith. A minor, narrow-gauge line in the same area whose route can still be traced was that opened about 1815 from the Melyngriffith works to Pentyrch forge.

The Aberdare canal had three ironworks lines which are still discoverable. The Hirwaun–Abernant tramroad (a 4 ft. 2 in. plateway of 1805) has left a bridge at Llwydcoed and sleeper blocks all along its four-mile course, including one unbroken run of at least a mile and a half, 620 ft. up, which Baxter considered 'undoubtedly the finest stretch of tramroad remaining': a shorter line of 1819 running south from the head-basin at Abernant can also be traced: and the Llwydcoed line proper completes the trio. Opened in 1811, this last has left sleepers at Aberdare and a single-span bridge over the Afon Cynon at Robertstown which is almost certainly the oldest extant iron railway bridge in the world (Plate 4). Indeed, its only known predecessor—a Scottish structure built a year earlier and destroyed in the present century—was a mere accessory to a stone bridge alongside.

The Treforest–Gyfeillon plateway of 1809, which connected with the Rev Dr Griffith's canal, was of three-foot gauge: it carried passengers in coal wagons returning empty, and its route can be traced. Smith's canal at Llansamlet connected with Scott's railway and indeed his colliery: opened in 1816, it has bequeathed an embankment at Birchgrove. And in the Port Talbot area the Cwmavon works line from Morfa Newydd to Bryn colliery, opened in 1819 to carry tin-plate as well as coal, has left a most notable five-arched bridge over the Avon as well as an incline at Mynydd Bychan.

A more extensive system, built as a 4 ft. 7 in. edgeway, served the harbour of Porthcawl. The main line of this—opened in 1828—ran for seventeen miles north to the Maesteg area: a general-purpose carrier of which most later became a conventional mineral railway, the Duffryn Llynvi and Porthcawl has bequeathed earthworks at Tondu and Llangynwyd and a bridge at Gelli-Las, and its curious 'sand-tunnel' at Porthcawl harbour can also still be traced. A connecting line running south from Park Slip, the Bridgend railway, was opened two years later: this has left the three-arched Glan Rhyd bridge over the river Ogmore (which is signed with the name of its mason, Morgan Thomas) and some sleeper blocks nearby.

The tunnel at Coytrahen belongs to a brickworks line of uncertain date; but before leaving these densely-knit valleys of Glamorgan which form the richest tramway country in Britain one other, if brief, 'independent' line should be mentioned. Serving the Rhyd-y-fen blast furnace, this ran two miles up the valley from Cwmavon. Its viaduct of about 1824 at Pont-rhyd-y-fen remains a striking structure.

Still deeper into Wales were the Llanelly edgeway in Carmarthenshire (a short limestone and coke line of 1833, running north from Machynys pool on the Burry, which has left an incline at Dafen) and the Carway line of 1802 or earlier which led from the Kidwelly and Llanelly canal at Bryn to nearby coal pits and from which there survives a bridge over the Gwendraeth Fawr river. Even Pembrokeshire had two tramways which have left traces, the five-mile Saundersfoot line of 1832 (a fish-bellied edgeway, laid on what is optimistically recorded as a gauge of 4 ft. 0⅜ in.) which carried minerals down to the harbour from north of Thomas Chapel and has left a self-acting incline at the port and a 400-yard tunnel under the present station, and the similar (but very late, for it was not opened until 1842) Wiseman's Bridge line with its bridge under the main road at Kilgetty and three short tunnels near the pleasantly-named Stepaside.

This may be the place to mention the other pre-1830 lines of the principality, even though these belong to a tradition somewhat different from those of Gwent. In Flint, for instance, there are traces of the short Aston Hall–Queensferry colliery line of 1801, and in Denbighshire of the line which linked the north side of Telford's great Pont Cysyllte aqueduct on the Llangollen canal to the collieries of Ruabon Brook. This last opened about 1806, was a three-foot edgeway, and has left bridges at Abernant and Cefn as well as at Pont Cysyllte itself. A little further west, remains of another system are to be found at Trevor (Plate 6).

An early (1801) example of the independent slate-carrying lines typical of North Wales ran south from Port Penrhyn near Bangor (Caernarvon) to the huge Bethesda quarries: over six miles long, of the 1 ft. 11 in. gauge which became typical of such systems, and laid with oval (or Wyatt's) rails, the traces of its first course comprise earthworks at Afon Ogwen and a bridge at Dinas Farm, whilst numerous relics of the system have been assembled at the Penrhyn Castle museum. From Port Dinorwic another slate line with a partly-traceable course—though this time a four-foot edgeway opened in 1824—ran south-east to Fachwen and has left inclines at Garth and Graig Llwyd. Until recently an interesting layout of sidings remained visible at the harbour; a tunnel which accepted narrow-gauge wagons off transporters is still there, and a brief length of track (though not the original) remains in use at the Dinorwic quarries.

Also in Caernarvonshire was the Nantlle railway of 1828 which ran for nearly nine miles south from Caernarvon harbour to the Gloddfarlon quarries. Although its major length was closed about a century ago and partly rebuilt as a conventional line, a mile or two east from Tal-y-Sarn remained in use for internal quarry transport as late as 1963 and track—again not the original—is still in place. The rest of the route is marked by a short tunnel at Coed Helen and the remains of a bridge over the Afon Seiont to the south of Caernarvon town, another ruined bridge at Bontnewydd, intact bridges at Plas Dinas and Nantlle, and an embankment at Bronydd.

On the border of this county and Merioneth a mile of track—probably of 3 ft. gauge—was about 1807 laid across the estuary of Portmadoc to assist in the building (and, later, maintenance) of William Madocks' Traeth

Mawr 'cob' or causeway: this was, of course, later to be incorporated into the Festiniog railway. Another Welsh line now used for pleasure also has origins in the same period, though only a half-mile of the later Welshpool and Llanfair light railway in Montgomeryshire was built as a canal feeder from the Stondart quarries before 1818 and this section, running through the town, has now been demetalled. A length of its interesting trackwork—chaired, and in the form of an inverted T—is preserved in the Science Museum, Exhibition Road, London, SW.

As has been noted, Monmouth, Hereford and Gloucester-beyond-the-Severn must be considered here together with South Wales. In the first of these counties a short line of 1829 with a dark but traversable tunnel at The Grove followed the Afon Llwyd at Pontypool, and from Half Way House near Cwmbran a four-mile line to the Usk at Caerleon was opened by 1801. This has left an intact overbridge at Lower Malthouse, Ponthir, the remains of other bridges at Llantarnam over the Avon Llwyd and at Ponthir, and earthworks at the latter place and at Greenmeadow. A short limestone line of about 1804 from Tredegar to Trevil has also left earthworks.

Nine miles north-west of Newport, and near Crosskeys, was a centre suitably known as Nine Mile Point. This formed a junction for a network of 4 ft. 2 in. plateways, totalling over fifty miles and including the first public line in Wales, which have left disappointingly few remains since they were later relaid as conventional railways: even the magnificent Risca viaduct on the Newport line of 1805 was destroyed at the start of the present century, a 900-yard tunnel lies buried under the slag-tips of Ebbw Vale, and, except for a section of dual-purpose rail preserved by the BRB, the Old Rumney and Sirhowy lines have vanished without trace. The Penilwyn or Llanarth tramroad of 1824 which ran north to Blackwood, however, has been more fortunate and has left bridge remains at Blackwood and Pontllanfraith and a series of sleeper blocks at the latter site.

Also in Monmouth were two other lines linked with the Brecknock canal—the seven-mile Llanvihangel railway of 1814 (a 3 ft. 6 in. plateway from Govilon, largely absorbed into a standard line, with earthworks at Pen-y-Worlodd) and its equally long continuation made five years later to Llangua bridge in Hereford. This, the Grosmont railway, has left a fifty-foot high embankment at Pandy.

From the 'independents' of the county the only dateable survivor is the remarkable and overgrown tunnel—for at over 2,000 yards it was easily the longest of its type when opened about 1815, though it came into being as an almost unintentional linking of mining passages—of the short, two-foot-gauge Pwlldu (earlier Tyla, and later Hill's) plateway from Blaenavon, though a much briefer tunnel nearby at Garn Ddyrys on Blorenge Mountain probably belongs to an extension of this system. But one river-linked line remains to be mentioned, the Monmouth railway from May Hill, Monmouth eastwards to Howler Slade in the Forest of Dean, Gloucestershire, which with its branches totalled some eleven miles. Opened in 1812 as a 3 ft. 6 in. general-traffic plateway, this was later authorised to carry passengers. It has left a fragment of an incline at Poolway near Coleford, another with an underbridge near Redbrook, the abutments of a bridge at Whitecliff, and the remains of a 330-yard tunnel at Newland: there are two other shorter tunnels which it is a challenge to discover, and the route can be traced through Coleford.

Back across the Wye in Herefordshire, the eleven-mile Hereford railway picked up the Grosmont line at Llangua and continued to the Wye bridge of Hereford itself: opened in 1829 and later in part adopted as a conventional railway, this was a 3 ft. 6 in. plateway carrying assorted minerals and (ten years later) passengers. Its remains include earthworks at Poplar Wood, Worm Brook and St Devereux, as well as the station-name 'Tram Inn'. The Kington railway, a similar but independent system opened between 1820 and 1825, ran from Eardisley (where it met the Hay line) to the Burlinjobb ironworks in Radnorshire: this has left a culvert at Eardisley, a stone bridge at Kington and the notable Waterloo iron bridge over the river Arrow, sleeper blocks near Hill House farm, and an attractive route alongside Offa's Dyke.

Gloucestershire had short lines linked primarily to the Wye, but these have now vanished. In the then roadless—and still densely-wooded and highly-individual—quarter of England called the Forest of Dean, however, there flourished two other sizeable 3 ft. 6 in. plateway systems—one totalling some sixteen miles, the other over thirty—whose history has filled several books.

Controversies remain to be settled, and perhaps discoveries to be made, concerning both of them: meanwhile, much is being lost through new industries and afforestation. But the survivors from the Bullo Pill railway of 1809, which ran west and then north from a wharf on the Severn of which traces remain to the Cinderford area and which was later named the Forest of Dean railway are still fairly extensive: they include earthworks at Bullo, the remains of a branch-line bridge near Lightmoor, and a noteworthy rebored tunnel 1,100 yards long at The Haie hill. (Plate 4). A shorter tunnel on another branch can be traced at Shakemantle; and in the Cinderford area there are a three-arched bridge, a milepost opposite the Methodist chapel at Cinderford Bridge, and traces of the stone blocks which can be found in several other locations but particularly across Bilson Green.

The fourteen-mile main line of the system of 1810 which was first known as the Lydney and Lydbrook and later as the Severn and Wye railway ran north from Lydney—where the harbour office dated 1813 survives—to Bishopswood in Herefordshire, and was hence directly connected to both boundary rivers of the Forest. From this system there remains a tunnel and traces of a wharf at Bishopswood and shorter tunnels near Dark Hill and (with a dated north portal) Yorkley, earthworks at Cannop and elsewhere, and stone blocks at Bishopswood, Parkend, Mireystock, Dark Hill, and other sites. On a branch at Lydbrook the former 'wire works' incline is traceable.

The last section of Severn and Wye track to remain *in situ* is reported to be a few yards on a bridge at Cannop Ponds near Parkend; but the Narrow Gauge Museum at Towyn, Wales, which is mentioned more fully in a later chapter, preserves specimens of two types of track as well as a rather decayed stone-carrying wagon. (A local enthusiast has also made a collection of relics from the Forest of Dean lines, the larger of which he has loaned to the museum of Tewkesbury, Glos.) Finally, large parts of these networks—as of some of the other substantial systems mentioned in this chapter—were of course later converted to conventional mineral lines or ordinary railways which remained in use until recently, and so lost much of their individuality.

To the many enthusiasts to whom the attraction of even a long-abandoned railway is inseparable from the remembered reek of steam coal, the foregoing pages may have seemed of interest to local antiquarians rather than transport-lovers, a catalogue coming to life only when dealing with a line close to the reader's own backyard or stumbled across on a holiday. But for the non-specialist these remains grow immensely in fascination when one clothes them with their landscape. Even at the time of Priestley's survey of 1830 this was essentially the landscape of the first enclosures, a world almost as remote from us today as that in which the cathedrals arose new-built and white; but it is broken here and there by an isolated blast-furnace or forge-hammer hidden in the woods, by the scar of a quarry incline high on a hillside or the drift of a coal shaft vanishing into an escarpment, by a textile mill standing four-square and seven stories high beside a fast-flowing river. And linking these to each other, to the staithes where narrow-boat or barge awaited, or to the blue-water harbours, there ran the tramroads—wooden and iron, edgeways and plateways, narrow-gauge and broad, timber-sleepered and stone-blocked, but with few exceptions still worked in the 1820s by the horses who plodded, head down, along some 1,500 miles of route.

In these terms, the classic tramway age—those sixty or seventy years of considerable if half-concealed industrial enterprise in which even the Napoleonic wars mark no sharp watershed—comes alive to the imagination. But the fact must not be lost sight of that, slow as progress in land transport proved to be, this *was* a period of transition from mediaeval to modern patterns of industry—and, in particular, from local to national concepts of communication. This chapter (and it is interesting to note that the gazetteer to it covers only about a third of the counties of England, the proportion being higher in Wales which owned over a quarter of Britain's tramway mileage and lower in Scotland) began with a line whose exceptional proprietors looked beyond their parish boundaries. Hence it can suitably end with two later railways which shared the feature that their economic justification did not rely primarily on trade originating from their terminals.

The older—and once again it is associated with a town remote from modern industry—was the Stratford-upon-Avon and Moreton railway of 1826. Despite its construction as a 4 ft. 8½ in. edgeway (though one possibly proceeded by a timber road), this was clearly one of the last of the classic tramways rather than a precursor of the railway age; but while its proprietors regarded it primarily as a feeder of agricultural produce and stone to the Stratford canal and the river Avon, they also looked in the opposite direction and believed that it would prove a link in a transport system reaching from Birmingham to London. In 1819, in fact, William James had surveyed the full length of such a route, this being the first survey ever conducted over so great a distance though only one of the many which James carried out at his own expense. In the event, however, it was not until the early '50s that the system was linked to lines approaching from the south and permission granted for passenger traffic.

The original line ran sixteen miles south from the Stratford canal basin to Moreton-in-Marsh, though a short spur later led to Shipston-on-Stour too. By 1870 the southernmost sections were being operated as part of a main-line railway and the tram road itself was abandoned. But the route is traceable throughout, and even apart from its antiquarian interest provides a most pleasant walk through the Stour valley.

To the south there are earthworks at Berry Field Farm and a bridge over the river at Talton: two other bridges follow. Further north beyond Alderminster the trace becomes road-shouldering; but it is still marked by a long cutting and embankment and finishes in splendid style as it sweeps into Stratford over the curved, Avon-spanning bridge of nine flattened brick arches of 35 ft. span, attributed to John Rastrick of Stourbridge, which must be the most graceful of all the memorials of the tramway age. (Plate 7). This is fully as worthy of preservation as Clopton bridge itself; and fortunately there can be no valid argument against this, since it provides a well-appreciated by-pass by which pedestrians can avoid the breath of those reeking tubes, the exhausts of automobiles jammed on the road-bridge Shakespeare knew.

Probably few of Stratford's tourists realise the origin of this amenity; but they have no excuse for not doing so, since many years ago the authorities installed an original wagon (Plate 3) and section of the light, fish-bellied wrought-iron track at the town end of the bridge, together with an explanatory plaque. (Another track section is preserved in the Leicester museum). Finally, the weigh-house subsists beside the canal basin, itself now pleasantly busy again with cruisers exploring the loveliest of all Britain's inland waterways; and this is as pretty a building as any in Stratford and a more sincere one than most. It is a fortunate town whose early incursions into industry did so much to adorn it.

The other tramway with through-route pretensions (and this was also a 4 ft. 8½ in. edgeway, using the obsolescent fish-bellied rails) was laid by Josias Jessop through the very different but equally memorable scenery of the High Peak, Derbyshire. Canals had approached this 1,000 ft.-high plateau, which had little to offer the outside world except limestone and the needs of its inhabitants, at Whaley Bridge on the west and Cromford on the east; but the massif itself remained six or seven hundred feet above access from either side. No fact brings alive the despair of early nineteenth-century Britain of achieving smooth bulk transport by land, and its according commitment to the waterways, than that the scheme of building a junction canal was seriously considered. Estimates for a tramway though were £150,000, less than a quarter of those for a canal.

Combined with the attraction of the limestone of the Peak itself was the possibility of forming a route from Manchester to London; and eventually it was realised that a combination of tramway and waterway would be an acceptable compromise. So there came into being in 1830 the Cromford and High Peak railway, which spanned 34 miles of central Derbyshire—and some of the highest country in England—under the motto *Divina Arte Palladis*. On the company's arms this learned slogan surrounded, not an owl, but a very humble wooden tramway wagon.

The High Peak line, though, had more 'artificial engines' than that, for inevitably it relied heavily on inclines to defeat the escarpments at either side and help it over its 1,266 ft. summit. At the eastern end these were four in number (all but one being powered), and of no more than the normal length of a few hundred yards. But height from Cromford was eventually gained mainly by two tremendous cable-ways, each about three-quarters of a mile long and over 400 ft. in height.

Steam locomotives were employed as early as 1834 on the C&HP, and passengers were regularly carried. This traffic did not cease until 1877, Frederick Williams being one of the last travellers. But the tramway obviously could not complete when such conventional lines as the Midland railway—to which it was itself linked by a short extension from Cromford wharf—entered the area; and a later competitor was the Ashbourne branch of the London and North Western, which company in fact acquired the tramway. Westward from Parsley Hay, which is itself about 1100 ft. up, this branch provided an incline-free route to Manchester, and the western section of the system was hence closed in the early 1890s.

Lengths even of this remained in use until recently, however; and in addition to the inclines its remains are hence considerable. Perhaps the most massive is the rebored Burbage tunnel, nearly 640 yards long: the lazy can obtain a panoramic view of this—and of a mile or so of the system—from the Canholes road junction on A53. A shorter tunnel—but one which has kept its original form—is to be found at Newhaven, and there are intact bridges at Horwich End (near the Whaley Bridge terminus), Fernilee, Bunsall Farm, Brier Low, Hurlow and elsewhere, as well as earthworks throughout the route.

The eastern end of the system was somewhat realigned and rebuilt at the same period. It did, however, preserve the flavour of an early-nineteenth-century tramway as it cut across the high plateau between drystone walls, carrying its limestone, its water for the farms, and its occasional passenger excursions.

In 1967 this unique link with the tramway past was at last closed; and all that is left now is to walk its trace. The starred attractions are, of course, the two great inclines, of which the higher—the Middleton incline proper—preserves not only the winding house (scheduled as an historic monument) but the original, five pounds-per-square-inch steam engine of about 1830. On the lower or Sheep Pastures incline—itself an amalgamation of two earlier ones—the motive power was replaced by electrical gear. But again the engine house, of a polygonal form perhaps inherited from the canal lock-cut cabins, is original, as are the offices at the foot of the run and close to the canal wharf.

Following an accident in which the cable broke and a rake of wagons jumped the terminus, the canal and the Midland main line before coming to rest beside the Derwent, this incline was provided with a remarkable safety system: the tracks were furnished with treadles which (through a wire-and-spiral-spring system of the type used to summon Victorian housemaids) ran a bell at regular intervals. Hearing this the pointsman closed a set of catch points. But if the tempo became *accelerando* he ran for his life, the system 'failed safe', and the wagons were directed into a stout underground bunker.

There was also, in place of any electrical link, a curious string-operated signalling system which owed more to the ship's telegraph than normal railway practice. It is to be hoped that these remain *in situ.* But no longer can Saturday-morning enthusiasts watch locomotives in steam being hauled up a 1/9 incline—or working gradients of up to 1/14 under their own power. And if ever there was a line which called for preservation through that blend of government support and enthusiasts' effort which reinstated the Stratford canal, then this is it.

Possibly over-much space has been devoted to these two systems, though both represent the tramroad in apotheosis and the second was remarkable by any standards. But together with the Surrey Iron railway they bracket the later tramway age in their chronology and show how the 'through-route' concept remained challenging, yet never fully realised, over thirty years. It is true, however, that so far rather more attention has been paid to the routes and civil engineering (if not the economic factors) of the tramway age than to its permanent way and rolling stock.

Even on lines where passengers were carried the latter never developed much beyond the form of a wooden-bodied open tub, later provided with wheels (and perhaps a frame or even sides) of iron. These sides might be vertical or of wheelbarrow form, divers types of couplings and brakes were tried, various systems of discharge—including bottom-hopper opening—were used, and local variants emerged such as the heavy stone-carrying wagons of the Prior Park line, the flat-cars of the Plymouth and Dartmoor or the high-sided and chariot-prowed coal chaldrons of the north-east. But the wain has hardly changed in basic form from the invention of the wheel to mineral wagons of a type still being built, and the examples already mentioned are hence typical of those of the whole tramway age.

For instance, another of the same school, now preserved by the BRB, came from the Belvoir Castle (Leics.) line. This was itself constructed in 1815 to link the Grantham canal to the Duke of Rutland's private coal-cellar, and was not finally closed until over a century later. Sections of the fish-bellied rail from it are preserved by the Science Museum, London, the BRB collection and the Leicester museum—even remain in place in His Grace's grounds. Stone sleepers and a building survive at Bottesford wharf near Muston, and much of the route can be followed.

With trackwork the position is more complex. This book has already remarked on the introduction of stone sleeper-blocks, which proved of doubtful advantage since their lack of resilience led to frequent fracture of the rails even after 1810 when (probably on the recommendation of William

James) wrought began to replace cast iron and so prepare the way for the locomotive age: experiments with cast-iron sleepers led to the same trouble. It has also noted the general dichotomy between the edgeway and the plate-way: the former became popular in the north and proved more amenable to systems with complexes of points and sidings, whilst the latter, favoured in the south, was supposedly stronger and had the rather illusory virtue that the wagons which worked plateways had unflanged wheels suitable for use on ordinary roads.

But these are only the main themes in the conflict of rail shapes, sizes and materials, and in the early nineteenth century re-layings became frequent. For example, oval edge-rails were favoured on some systems, particularly in conjunction with double-flanged wheels. Fish-bellying was resorted to for both the plate and bar types: various forms of chairs and dovetailing were employed, special patterns of track were resorted to at level crossings or to allow of use by more than one type of wagon, and throughout the period there was a tendency towards heavier sections in greater lengths as the haulage of single wagons or small groups of them gave place to the working of real trains. Even continuously-welded track was proposed by John Birkinshaw in 1820, and there were at least two monorail systems—one of which carried passengers—in use by 1826.

With so much variety of form and local preference the study of early rails has remained a somewhat specialised one, and has not been helped by the widely-dispersed nature of the relics and the fact that the BRB has necessarily paid comparatively little attention to pre-1830 relics. A number of examples which either remain *in situ* or have been transferred to museums have, of course, been mentioned above; but even reputable museums are sometimes uncertain as to the provenance of relics of this type and tend to leave them to gather dust in what are euphemistically known as reserve collections. In any case the list cannot yet be complete, other interesting relics remain in private hands, and there are certainly a number of short lengths of track still waiting to be identified in the backyards of unsuccessful north-country factories.

Since old tracks are usually unearthed in runs of fair length and only a yard or two suffices to show their features, it should be possible to build up a reasonably representative central collection whilst still leaving samples in regional museums or on original sites. Meanwhile, the finest collection of British rail lengths is reported lost in Cairo and, as Baxter wrote, "there is a real need to locate, collate and catalogue all the sundry items of early rails and other tramroad relics preserved in various hands up and down the country and . . . to ensure that their whereabouts are known and that their permanent preservation is ensured."

It is hoped that the foregoing chapters have at least contributed towards that end.

# PART TWO

# *THE RAILWAY SCENE*

## *IV TRANSITION*

THE TRAMWAY age did not suddenly end in 1830. A number of later lines which were tramways in the sense that they were built with light engineering to serve local needs and used horse traction to haul specialised loads have already been mentioned; and others were built as late as 1852, when there was opened the three-foot-gauge Moel-y-Fan feeder to Pentre Felin at the Llangollen canal-head—probably the last line to be laid on stone-block sleepers, and one which has bequeathed an incline and earthworks at Hendy in the Valle Crucis. Typical of those which have left substantial remains are the Coleorton or Lount line in Leicestershire which is still worked by the National Coal Board (1833), the Storeton and perhaps the Poynton in Cheshire (about 1838), and the line inland from Par in Cornwall (about 1840) whose ten-arched and emblazoned granite Treffry viaduct is 650 ft. long and has been described by Eric Newby as 'of Piranesian grandeur'. The upper level of this last structure carried a china-clay line and the lower—still functioning—formed an aqueduct to provide power for the water-wheels of Fowey.

Another line which must be included here is the Festiniog in Merioneth (Wales). Its antecedents as a contractor's adjunct to the Portmadoc causeway have already been mentioned; but in 1836 this section was relaid on a 1 ft. 11½ in. gauge (though not yet with modern-style rails) and the line was continued to the Blaenau Ffestiniog slate quarries fourteen miles distant, a remarkable feature of the engineering being that a gentle uphill gradient was preserved all the way to aid gravity-working. This sinuous line has, of course, been reopened for the pleasure of tourists and railway-lovers; and though a new alignment has had to be adopted for the northern half, the earthworks and structures (including the Boston Lodge workshops) as far as Tan-y-Bwlch are substantially those of 1836.

The narrow-gauge tradition was continued by a number of lines, particularly in North Wales. But fascinating as many of these post-1830 tramways, light railways and mineral lines remain, they are divergers from the main line of transport development. They and their remains are perhaps of curiosity value rather than true historic importance, though they form a bridge to the passenger-carrying light railways mentioned in later chapters.

For by now railways proper were being constructed. It is typical of this period of transition, for instance, that between 1825 and 1830 an average of half a dozen railway Acts was being passed every year. Many of the projected lines were never realised; but those which were divide almost equally into late tramways such as the Rhymney and the Hereford and true general-purpose railways such as the St Helens and Runcorn Gap, the Garnick and Glasgow (with an embankment still in use at Robroyston Moss), and the Leicester and Swannington (Plate 7)—a collection of relics from which last, whose mile-long tunnel at Glenfield has left ventilating shafts in several back gardens and whose incline house can still be seen at Bagworth, can be be found in the Leicester museum. Even before 1820 it was becoming realised that the concept of a railway was synthesised from a number of themes which have already been mentioned in this book, such as the use of a chaired or flat-bottomed edge-rail (probably laid to a 4 ft. 8½ in. gauge and *not* on sleeper blocks, though these remained in use on the Bodmin and Wadebridge line as late as 1895), common-carrier and passenger-haulage rights, and parliamentary recognition. But central to it now was the use of locomotive power.

The energy of steam was not linked to the convenience and economy of a railed track before 1800; but five years after that date stationary engines began to be introduced on the inclines which were so typical a feature of the tramway systems. These latter, in fact, temporarily regained popularity at the expense of devious and gently-graded lines with the coming of steam power; for instance, Stephenson's Whitby and Pickering (Yorks) line of 1836, though in some respects a true railway, had an incline near Goathland, and for a number of years more these remained common features at city termini.

Even in a number of cases where dateable powered inclines survive, however, it is not always clear whether the ruined stone building seen half-way up a Welsh mountain-side was an enginehouse or simply a weigh-office. Equally uncertain are the positions of the engines used for cable-haulage on the level on Benjamin Thompson's system, though this method of traction was used on railways such as the London (Fenchurch St) and Blackwall and the Durham and Sunderland as late as the 1840s and it is possible that sites can be identified on the Brunton and Shields and some neighbouring lines. But a number of winding-engines of both types have been preserved, and form striking examples of early nineteenth century engineering if only marginally railway exhibits.

Such eccentric experiments in locomotion as sail-driven craft and engines which propelled themselves on legs or chains have vanished with no more trace than Trevithick's 'Catch me who Can' track where the forecourt of Euston now stands, though the Blenkinsop-Murray rack system proved more enduring and was used on the Middleton line up to 1835. But essentially, the first three decades of the last century were those which saw the development and eventual triumph of what was to become the conventional steam locomotive.

For the experiments of Trevithick at Penydarren, of Stephenson at Killingworth and of William Hedley and the Blackett school at Wylam were not unique, and on perhaps a dozen other tramways previously mentioned (distributed from Scotland to Somerset, but almost all of the waterway-linked type) locomotive traction was intermittently used in the period 1800–1830. In most cases, even when the tram engine itself did not explode, it proved too heavy for track laid for horse haulage and the marriage was soon dissolved; and it is hence more surprising that a later chapter dealing with locomotives in retirement can begin in earnest as early as 1829 than that only two immortals survive from *before* that date. But the present brief chapter is concerned with the transition from tramway to railway, with their overlapping and their co-existence. And no more transitional line could be found that the Stockton and Darlington (Co. Durham), which was opened to traffic in 1825.

This was built under a Parliamentary Act which empowered it to carry passengers, was laid by George Stephenson on a trace which involved fairly massive earthworks, emerged after some debate as an edgeway on a gauge of 4 ft. 8 in. (only fifteen years later was the extra half-inch added), and used locomotives from the start; in all these respects the twenty-seven-mile system was a true railway. But Tees-side cannot claim to be the birthplace of the railway any more unambiguously than Tyneside can claim the tramway; for the line also relied almost entirely on serving local collieries (into which several short branches ran), was laid on stone sleepers, and used horses for its passenger traction—perhaps wisely, since two early locomotives exploded and *Periculum Privatum Utilitas Publica* was its disturbing motto. And in these respects it looked back to the past.

The familiar term 'Stockton and Darlington' is in fact a slight misnomer. The time-honoured names of many transport enterprises frequently overshoot the terminus actually achieved; but in some cases they are litotic rather than hyperbolic, and from its start the S&D continued its westward run from the Tees estuary in a more northerly direction to Witton Park colliery, which is north of Bishop Auckland and hence as far again beyond Darlington. Since the stretch between the two name-towns has remained in use (though with continual rebuildings), it is on this by-passed extension that most of the relics of its original state are to be found. There are, for instance, earthworks at Phoenix Row, Low Etherley and North Leaze as well as the substantial, stone-blocked remains of two powered inclines at Brusselton (Plate 8) and Etherley. Nearby, Shildon became the site of the world's first factory—still in use by BR—devoted mainly to the building of locomotives and rolling stock.

The railway museum at York preserves two relics of the system. Of its stock there is a chaldron wagon dating from 1828; and the structure of the unusual little bowstring iron bridge which until 1901 crossed the river Gaunless near West Auckland—where the abutments remain *in situ*—has been re-erected there too. Also over the Gaunless, but on a branch-line, there was built in stone from a full-sized timber model a skewed bridge believed to be the first of its kind in the world.

Since a similar claim can be made for the iron bridge, these are important relics. But just as important as them, or as Ignatius Bonomi's three-arched stone bridge of 1825 which crosses the Skerne at North Road, Darlington

(Plate 8); this, perhaps the first bridge of the railway age, has been widened, but the south side shows the original work), is the fact that in Bridge Road, St Johns, Stockton-on-Tees, there is a now-uninhabited cottage beside a level crossing with a plaque which states that from it there were sold, for the first time in the world's history, tickets for passengers wishing to travel by rail.

This 'precious relic' (as David Lloyd describes it) was not yet quite a station: like several private houses, inns, toll-booths and wharfs close to early tracks it had no real provision for the 'booking' of passengers, and it could be argued that the station is the one major item in the modern concept of a railway which was unknown before 1830. Not until 1842, in fact, did the S&D acquire a true station such as still exists (almost in its original state, and still handling a few local trains) at North Road, Darlington. But the Stockton building took the railways one step further towards that state in which motive power and rolling stock must be considered separately from the structures of the civil engineers and from the railway architecture which was so soon to take shape in the custom-built station.

PLATE 9

Among the earliest bridges of the railway age are Brunel's spanning the Thames at Maidenhead (top) and Stephenson's over the A5 at Denbigh Hall (above). The foundations in front of this are those of the 'mean alehouse' which served as a temporary terminus for the line; (left) gives an unusual view of Rastrick and Mocatta's Ouse viaduct at Balcombe, Sussex.

PLATE 10

Stephenson's tubular bridges on the way to Holyhead. The Britannia at Menai (above left) is guarded by four lions (above) by John Thomas—'of the antique, knocker-nosed, pimple-faced Egyptian form', according to a contemporary account. Conway (below) with Telford's road suspension bridge in the background, wears mediaeval armour.

PLATE 11

Artistry in stone and iron. Above, the Royal Border bridge at Berwick is being crossed by a special football train. Below, the floodlit Royal Albert bridge at Saltash.

PLATE 12

The disused bowstrong bridge over the Tyne near Wylam (top), the Ballochmyle viaduct south of Glasgow (above) and the skewed bridge across the disused canal at Todmorden, Yorks (left) are all in their ways noteworthy.

PLATE 13

Two late Scottish estuary-bridges—the Tay (above), showing the piers of its tragic predecessor, and the Forth (left top). The Liskeard viaduct in Cornwall (left below) is also flanked by earlier piers, in this case from Brunel's timber structure. All but the right-hand trusses of the Barmouth estuary bridge (below) remain of wood.

PLATE 14

Cast-iron craftsmanship is displayed in Andrew Hankyside's intricate work at Friargate, Derby (above left) and the finials of Blackfriars bridge, London (above right). The present state of a Border-country viaduct across the Tweed (below) reveals the fate of many fine structures.

PLATE 15

Fortified tunnel-portals at Grosmont on Stephenson's abandoned Whitby and Pickering line (top), Shugborough, Staffs. (centre) and Red Hill, Notts. (bottom).

PLATE 16

Tunnel details—(above) the arms of Lord Braybrook on the south portal at Audley End, and (below) one of the ventilating shafts which march across Blea Moor on the Settle and Carlisle line.

# V CIVIL ENGINEERING

It has been seen that, in the department of the civil engineer at least, the tramway age had supplied the early railway age with almost its full repertoire of devices and techniques. Embankments and cuttings made well before 1830 were indeed adopted by the Victorian companies; and these were to be bequeathed a century later to British Railways, which in some cases they still serve with only minor strengthenings.

The following thirty years—and particularly the late 1830s and early 1840s—were, however, to add so many more such structures that the national trunk railway system still largely runs over the foundations of that period. Between 1830 and 1860, for instance, over 25,000 bridges were built, more than had existed in the whole kingdom before: today's total of railway bridges is about 60,000 (plus around a thousand tunnels), and to the satisfaction of those with an affection for the past it would take several generations to replace all these Victorian relics even at BR's present fairly energetic rate of progress. Partly thanks to the low cost of labour then prevailing, the nineteenth-century engineers, even more than their predecessors, built such works with generous factors of safety, so that Brunel's leaping Thames bridges and the cuttings and tunnels of the Stephensons have needed only routine servicing to keep them fit for an age when train speeds and axle-loadings both average more than twice that of the traffic they were designed to bear—and when total train weights have increased by an even greater ratio.

Hence there is little in this field which can be classed as a relic in the sense of something outlived, set apart and deliberately preserved. The railway engineering of up to a century ago, like the ecclesiastical architecture of up to five centuries ago, exhibit a perfect synthesis of purpose, design and materials and forms part of the function-serving scene of Britain today: *si monumentum requiris, circumspice.* Even where early lines have recently been abandoned their earthworks and their brick or masonry arches (though not, unfortunately, their metal structures) generally survive, if only because it would prove too expensive to blow them up.

The earlier Victorian railway works, indeed, are not only likely to provide the sub-structure for any future form of guided transport, but are better equipped to survive atomic bombing than anything built in the present century save a few miles of motorway. Designed by a handful of largely self-taught men (who themselves recognised a herculean quality in their work, even if they did not realise that they were the last heirs of the renaissance tradition), thrown up or carved out in months—when funds permitted—by Thomas Brassey's gangs of navvies working with virtually no powered aids, many of them will probably still mark the face of Britain at Judgement Day.

Yet life-assured, ubiquitous and largely repetitive as they are, a number of these achievements call for special attention. The earliest date from George Stephenson's general-purpose Liverpool and Manchester railway of 1830—that 31-mile line of double-tracked, wrought-iron edgeway which, though originally laid largely on stone blocks, stands in relation to the Stockton and Darlington (to paraphrase Dendy Marshall) as a butterfly to a grub. Rainhill, and the site of Mr Huskisson's unfortunate death at Parkside which is marked by a memorial, are today little more than names lost in a conurbation, and even Chat Moss—though still forming a sinister and treacherous-looking gap amid the sprawling towns—nowadays appears dreary rather than historic. But the view from the Sankey valley up seventy feet to the nine-arched, stone-faced viaduct at Earlestown has changed little between the age of Ackermann prints and that of a.c. traction; and this forms as good a place as any to reflect that, commonplace as such 'stupendous edifices' were to become even a decade later, their building was almost miraculous in the context of their time, its tools and its knowledge. Not even Rome has set to work on such a scale.

The L&M alignment also included a tunnel as part of its rather complex terminal arrangements in the Edge Hill area; and since most of the rival claimants to the 'first railway' title lacked such a feature, the approach to the present Lime Street, Liverpool, station has a right to be considered the world's first true railway tunnel. A mile in length this was still short by comparison with a number of canal works; but being of adequate bore to accept later traffic it remains much as it did when the inaugural trains were cable-hauled through its gaslight on that bright morning of 15 September 1830 when flags, cannon and the Duke of Wellington saluted the opening of the railway age.

Though the associated Olive Mount rock cutting—that "awful chasm" which forms part of a series two miles long and up to 100 feet deep and was so dramatically featured in early lithographs is now some four times its original breadth (these widenings, indeed, led to a church being moved thrice over), and the arch in a Moorish style which did *not* become a regular feature of the railway scene has long been demolished, it does not need a great deal of imagination here to recollect that this line is considerably more than just another way through industrial Lancashire and that (for instance) the Sankey viaduct with its piers tapering as they rise to semicircular or segmental arches—these proportions being later exaggerated by Brunel into an almost Egyptian style—was to provide a prototype for railway engineers for three quarters of a century. There is also a smaller viaduct at Newton-le-Willows, a good example of a sharply-skewed bridge at Rainhill, and a three-mile system of tunnels under Liverpool connecting with the docks. Not in England only, but in every country in Europe and every continent in the world, British builders were to follow such forms.

Even George Stephenson, however, belonged in part to the tramway age. His son was to be almost exclusively a railway engineer; and it is Robert's signature which remains clear on the much larger enterprise which followed after a few years had passed and Britain had entered the age of Victoria. This was the first of those trunk lines whose realisation had challenged engineers for four decades and one whose length of well over a hundred miles Robert Stephenson perambulated more than twenty times, the London and Birmingham railway of 1838 with its ruling gradient of 1/330 and its realisation—for the greater part—of a modern type of track.

Bridges on this have recently been modified for electrification, though two very interesting ones survive over the A5 at Denbigh Hall (a temporary terminus of the line—Plate 9) and nearby over the Grand Union canal. But the cuttings east of Tring, Herts, (two-and-a-half miles through chalk up to 60 ft. deep) and at Roade, Northants, (one-and-a-half miles through sandstone reaching a depth of nearly 70 ft.), the Boxmoor embankment near Hemel Hempstead, and the six-arched viaduct across the Buckinghamshire Ouse at Wolverton are only the most notable of a large number of little-changed works along what was to become, in more than one sense, the premier line. And here too there is a notable tunnel, nearly a mile and a half long and set at Kilsby, Northants, in a historic crossroads of transportways south of Rugby. The diameter of its twin ventilating shafts—which are sixty feet across, the length of a modern passenger coach—has rather oddly been attributed to Stephenson's anxiety to provide an escape for flood water since the tunnel (which cost a third of a million pounds) was cut through quicksands. Some of the shorter tunnels are interesting in that the curved buttresses or horizontal arches of their portals recall the graceful 'turnover' bridges of the canals.

In the south of England, Kent pioneered the railway age with the Canterbury and Whitstable line opened in May, 1830. This was another which had been planned by the energetic William James; like such contemporaries as the St Helens railway it used stone sleepers, and it is noteworthy that in its woodland run of nearly seven miles it had no intermediate stations. (It was indeed a feature of the tramways, today reverted to as BR policy, that rail transport was conceived in terms of terminal points: the staffing of hopeful halts to generate business was only economic in terms of the Victorian equation of railways with passenger travel). Indeed, the C&W only had one real station—now vanished—since it petered out at the port in quayside tracks. It was abandoned even before the Beeching era; but its Tyler Hill tunnel remains, shorter than the Liverpool one with its bore of just under half-a-mile but possibly a few months senior in terms of the first traffic worked through. Here too, cable haulage was employed.

London's own first railway was not opened until 1836 and ran from near London Bridge to Deptford (and later Greenwich) over a viaduct of 878 brick arches still heavily used. But it was another suburban line which was extended by Rennie and Rastrick before 1841 to run over the fifty miles from south London to Brighton on a ruling gradient of 1/265.

Three sections of this route, which is today something between a main line and a commuter corridor, are of particular interest. At Merstham (where it runs alongside the Brighton road and the trace of the Surrey Iron Railway's extension), deep chalk cuttings comparable to the Tring ones, flank a mile-long tunnel under the North Downs. Duplicated at the end of the century for political as well as operating reasons this tunnel was, like several of its contemporaries, whitewashed and gaslit in its early years; it is today marked by a line of brick drums at the tops of its ventilating shafts. The corresponding tunnel under the South Downs at Clayton—the scene of an historic accident—has an ornate north portal; and between these a shorter tunnel through the Weald leads to the Italianate pavilions and balustrades of Moccata and Rastrick's very elegant viaduct of 37 brick and stone arches over the Sussex Ouse near Balcombe. (Plate 9)

This complex can hardly be glimpsed from the windows of a Brighton non-stop, and deserves suitably admiring walks. These might even suggest that a date around 1838 could be taken as the birth-year of conscious transport architecture. Earlier canal, tramway and railway works had, of course, had their own functional graces, and here and there armorial symbolism might have been added to a portal, an over-bridge built in a style dictated by a local landowner, or a terminal point given special treatment. But something more self-regarding was now taking shape.

So at Balcombe it is possible to see style treated for the first time—and for better or worse—as a factor deliberately added to routine railway structures. It is also possible that architectural embellishment is one of the few contributions made by the south to the railway scene, since even Stephenson and Budden were more tempted towards ornament (though in classic styles) at Watford and Primrose Hill than at portals further north. It was only at a later date that Midlands tunnels such as Shugborough, Staffs (1847—Plate 15) were tricked out in fantasticated styles; and even in this case the castellated west and the Egyptian east portals—both crowned with earlier follies—were only built in such elaborate forms to satisfy the taste of the Earl of Lichfield who also insisted on decorative bridges. The ornate portals of Clay Cross, Derby and at Red Hill south of the Trent however, date from as early as 1840, and that at Grosmont, Yorks, is earlier still. (Plate 15)

This desire for elegance also appears on another prototype line of the south—Isambard Kingdom Brunel's splendidly-aligned if unconventional trunk route to Bristol, commenced in 1836 and completed in 1841, whose gradients were for nearly ninety miles restricted to 1/750. (A section of the GWR's 'bridge' rails and longitudinal sleepers, though of standard gauge can be located near Gloucester station). This route's twin-span, red-brick bridges at Maidenhead (Plate 9), Moulsford and Basildon have already been referred to: the 128 ft. arches of the first of these were, however, widened some forty years later, as (and more clumsily) was the eight-arched Wharncliffe viaduct of stock-brick and stone over the Brent at Hanwell, Middlesex. The tree-mile curved embankment before Chippenham and the cutting at Sonning are also landmarks of the line. But perhaps the outstanding work is once again a tunnel—the bore, just under two miles in length and hence the longest of its age, at Box, east of Bath just in Wiltshire.

Certain portals of both this and the Middlehill or Twerton approach tunnel are dressed up in imposing Tudor-portcullis style, though those nearer Bristol are more straightforward in treatment. (Rather charmingly, though, one of these is decorated by a couple of fossils excavated by Brunel). The west entry to the longer tunnel, though chaste, is particularly impressive since it was close to the turnpike road, outlined against green hills, and so provided an advertisement site for the Great Western which could suggest that tunnel-travel was a joy rather than a death-trap: one medical opponent, however, still regarded Box as 'monstrous and extraordinary, most dangerous and impracticable'. After some 130 years of exposure, however, the sherry-pale Bath stone is beginning to show the effects of weather. Since it is unlikely that BR will be willing to find the money (even if it could find the masons) to restore such features, there is a clear case here—as wherever relics of the pristine state of Britain's first great railways are crumbling away—for *ad hoc* grants from the national purse.

The Great Western's rival—Joseph Locke's London and Southampton route, opened in 1840—is mainly remarkable for the fifteen-mile series of cuttings and embankments through chalk which hold its ruling gradient down to 1/250 in the Micheldever area between Basingstoke and Winchester. These have, in fact, been claimed to form the most massive cut-and-fill project in the world. But from the point of view of sheer cussedness in construction, none of the works mentioned above can compare with the 'old' Woodhead tunnel which ran for just on three miles—and over 950 ft. up—through the shale and grit-stone of the spine of England.

The line it serves, which was built to form a second link between Manchester and the West Riding cities (the earliest being Stephenson's valley-following Lancashire and Yorkshire route of 1838, whose only work is the Todmorden viaduct though there also survives an interesting iron bridge to the south at Slade (Plate 12) and a cutting and lengthy tunnel at Littleborough), is at present electrified. It was not the first to be engineered through mountainous country. But its sole predecessor in this field was another Stephenson line, the Newcastle and Carlisle of 1836 which again avoided major engineering works except for the Corby viaduct at Wetherby, Cumberland.

Both the original bore of the Woodhead tunnel—which was commenced by Charles Vignoles and completed by Joseph Locke in 1845 after seven years of struggle and its pioneer's fall from fame and fortune—and its slightly later duplicate, each of which cost about £200,000 as well as numerous lives, have now been abandoned for railway purposes and replaced by the double-track tunnel which should have been built in the first instance. Furthermore, with their stark air-shafts and fairly severe ornamentation only at the west end, these offer even less to the sightseer or industrial archaeologist than do the line's bridges across the Etherow near Broadbottom (1842) and the Dinting Vale (1844). (Both of these were originally built in timber, but only the piers survive from the first structures and even the later iron girders have to be propped intermediately.) But Woodhead, uniting Yorkshire with, rather unexpectedly, Cheshire, *was* the first mountain tunnel in the world, and for several decades the longest. For a number of years, indeed, it remained the longest of any type.

By 1842, after little more than ten years of construction, there were over 1,600 route miles of railway open in Britain—about the same as the total length of track achieved in the two centuries of the tramway age or of the canal mileage built in seventy years. And though several railways before the Edinburgh and Glasgow with its 36-arched viaduct (at Clifton Hall) had been opened in Scotland, and the Taff Vale and other heavily-engineered lines existed in Wales, nine tenths of this mileage was to be found in England.

There, in addition to the routes already mentioned, railways had been or were being built to link Manchester with Birmingham, Chester and Lancaster in the shape of the London and North Western system. Notable viaducts here are that of 1841 which marches above the Gustave Doré roofs of Stockport, another of twenty sandstone arches which crosses the river Weaver at Dutton and was built (in 1837) by Joseph Locke and *not* the Stephensons, and the companion to this at Penkridge. Other lines were to be found in the Hull and Derby areas—where thay would form the nuclei of the later North-Eastern and Midland networks respectively—and from Birmingham towards the south-west. George Stephenson's North Midland railway between Derby and the West Riding had produced some fine engineering as well as the elegant stations mentioned later and was also the scene of the first use of block signalling; and there were yet other lines about to operate in the eastern counties and from London to the channel ports of Dover and Folkestone.

In that bastion of Britain, William Cubitt's viaduct and embankment still bridge the Foord gap behind Folkestone, and the courses of his Abbotscliffe and Shakespeare's Cliff tunnels are marked by ventilation galleries opening to the sea as well as by shafts which, in these years of electrification, appear as forlorn as the relics of Cornish copper mines. A third cliff was shot away with one great blast of ten tons of powder, whose firing by the navy was treated as a public spectacle, and the sea-wall is also a pioneering work. Offshore lie the guarded headings made for the channel tunnel more than forty years later and eighty years ago.

Meanwhile, Brunel had in 1841 passed under an elegant road bridge at Uphill, Som, and was pressing on to Exeter, reached in 1844; in 1846 he would challenge the channel storms with his sea-wall under the red cliffs of Dawlish. Near to the home of railways at Low Lambton, Co. Durham, where the estate of the earl who pioneered Canada's independence ironically faces the ancestral home of George Washington's family, a notable stone viaduct of four main arches—the largest of them 160 ft. across and 125 ft. high—had been opened in 1838 as the Victoria Bridge: designed by the Newcastle architect, Benjamin Green, this is supposed to have been modelled on the great Roman work at Alcantara but also bears a family resemblance to the Causey arch. Yet the pace of construction, which had hitherto swallowed up the new richness of the nation almost as fast as the railways themselves had generated it, was now beginning to slow down. And in 1844 later national economics brought it to a temporary halt.

The railway age was, in the broadest sense, still only beginning; for route mileage was to treble in the next decade and increase more than tenfold to its maximum by the end of the century. But it is generally true that the majority of works built after this mid-forties period of taking stock—which was itself to be followed by the great investment mania and crash—not only lack the historic interest of the prototypes mentioned above but are less impressive in themselves.

Many such lines (such as the later trans-Pennine routes and those in Scotland) traversed wilder and more beautiful country than did their predecessors, and through the loneliness of their sites alone imposed great difficulties on their builders. But by the time they were constructed both locomotives and men's faith in them had so increased in power that routes did not need to be so easily graded and 1/50 was considered a reasonable figure. With money in short supply, branch lines reverted to devious, contour-following traces; and even on major railways such as the Great Northern civil engineers now felt themselves involved in a routine skill rather than a heroic venture. Except perhaps for one line (J. S. Crossley's Settle and Carlisle of 1875, marked by the deep Blea Moor tunnel (Plate 16) and Batty Moss viaduct whose engineering in masonry remains throughout as noteworthy as its landscape, but which may not remain open at the date of its centenary) and certainly in one department, the monumental age was over.

Hence only a handful more of the works executed in earth, stone or brick and dating from after 1840 need be mentioned here. A few, however, are outstanding. Among the viaducts, for instance, there remains Rastrick's curved and 27-arched span which takes the cross-country line to Lewes across the valley of the London–Brighton road which it crosses on a wider central arch: this structure of 1846 showed its strength when bombed nearly a century later. A combination of 2,250 ft. of earthworks and 1,275 ft. of 82 brick arches, completed as late as 1878 by Crossley and Barlow and now used only by freight tracks, spans the Welland valley between Seaton and Harringworth, Northants: this is the longest such overland structure in Britain, and so it is pleasant to find much of it in England's smallest county, Rutland.

Thomas Bouch's slender and lofty ten-arched viaduct of 1858 at Hownes Gill in remote country south of Consett, Co. Durham—which is built in the unusual material of firebrick—and those at Welwyn (1850, with forty arches up to 90 ft. high), at Crimple near Harrogate (1848), across the Calder at Whalley, Lancs (1848), and at Chappel in Essex, where Peter Bruff's 32 arches of 1849 make a fine gesture towards the classic orders, are also of more then common interest; whilst in Scotland the 180 ft. central span of the red sandstone bridge at Ballochmyle, Ayr, (Plate 12) was opened in 1848. This remained fifty years later the longest railway arch of masonry in the world: today its maximum of 164 ft. above the valley floor regrettably gives it the alternate distinction of being the highest bridge in Britain, since the two which over-topped it have now been destroyed.

Tunnels, too, can hardly be dismissed without mention of the portalless canal bores between Higham and Strood in Kent (1824), which were converted to railway use twenty years later. The Potters Bar series north of London, whose construction in 1850 is still remembered by the local name 'Spoil Bank Wood', the now-by-passed Harecastle group in the north Midlands (1848), the three-mile Standedge ('down south'—1849), Brunel's fine series of the early 1850's on the Chippenham-Weymouth line (such as Poundbury, which was sited so as to avoid prehistoric earthworks); Audley End on the way to Cambridge (1844: Plate 16) and the extension of the Midland railway to Manchester, whose now-demetalled tunnels of 1867 in the Dove Holes area were so frequent as to give the line the nickname of 'the flute', are also worth note. Scotland's oldest railway tunnel (1841) is the north bore of Haymarket, Edinburgh; but the Scotland Street tunnel in the same city wins for oddity value. At Bramhope (Yorks) on the Harrogate line a two-mile tunnel of 1849 has impressive shafts and an ornate north portal reproduced, as a memorial to the men killed in its construction in Otley churchyard.

But pride of place here must be given to the much later shaft below the Severn which was opened in 1886, two years after a rival company to the Great Western had bridged the estuary. At four-and-a-half miles, this double-tracked bore which involved thirteen years of struggle and the expenditure of well over a million pounds is still the longest underwater rail tunnel in the world. Some of the pumping and ventilating machinery of the age of Daniel Gooch remained in use at Sudbrook, Mon, until very recently; and though much of it has been sold for scrap, survivors can be found in the collections of the Science Museum, London, the National Museum of Wales, Cardiff, and the Industrial Museum of South Wales, Swansea. The course of a light railway used in the construction of the tunnel can still be traced at Portskeweth.

In one direction, too, the heroic age was in the late 1840s only beginning—the direction of building great bridges across coastal inlets. The favoured material, which had itself been developed to meet the needs of high-pressure boilers, now consisted of wrought iron plates riveted together by Fairbairn's hammers; but this had never yet been tested on a large scale. And little could speak more for the quality of Robert Stephenson than that at this time he was involved simultaneously in two schemes for the extension of existing lines in directions where the country inland was so rugged that coastal routes implying long trans-estuarine bridges were the natural first choice. These routes—both serving capital cities—ran northward from Doncaster to Edinburgh and westward from Chester (on an alignment which demanded the building not only of a sea-wall but of 'avalanche' protection) to Holyhead, the traditional port for Dublin.

Each of these enterprises involved two tideway crossings. One of the first to be opened—in the autumn of 1849—was the High Level bridge spanning the Tyne at Newcastle. In addition to its other features of interest, this is the only surviving bridge in which cast iron—a material which, as the collapse of a Stephenson bridge at Chester in 1847 had made clear, was not suitable for the construction of long girders—was widely used. It is also the earliest example of a dual-purpose type of structure which was to become more popular overseas, for the three-tracked railway was (and is) carried on a deck laid over the top of six tied-in or 'bowstring' arches, each of 125 ft. span, which have a roadway slung beneath them.

In the next year Queen Victoria opened what was described as 'the last act of the Union', the Royal Border bridge which spanned the Tweed and hence joined England and Scotland at Berwick—that half-independent city which had been the scene of some of Scotland's first railway experiments. Unusually for an estuarine structure—and presumably because the Tweed was not navigable for large craft—this bridge whose construction involved a peak labour force of nearly 2,750 men is a masonry one, built on piles driven as one of the first tasks of Nasmyth's steam hammer. O. S. Nock, describing it as 'a superb example of Robert Stephenson's work', continues 'In a beautiful setting between the heights . . . and the red-roofed town of Berwick, it carries the railway high above the winding estuary . . . the rails being 126 feet above high water mark. The bridge is built partly on a curve, and its twenty-eight warm red arches are finely seen from a northbound train.' (Plate 11)

As has been mentioned, Stephenson was at the same time building along the north Welsh coast—though here with the assistance of Joseph Fairbairn. His 425 ft. bridge, also of 1849, across the Conway estuary (Plate 10) below the castle has been attacked for its array in a full mediaeval rig of machicolations and arrow-slits, but these were wished on Stephenson by the city fathers. It is, indeed, interesting to note that by the middle of the century even the fastnesses of North Wales had read their Walter Scott and become mediaevally inclined.

In any case this sugar-icing does not affect the architectural merit of the bridge itself, which represents a brilliant solution of the problem of spanning a wide opening at a constant level. At Newcastle Stephenson has used flattened arches whose lateral thrusts were contained by tie-rods, and at Berwick a conventional stone viaduct. Here he adopted a third course—the building of a simple girder bridge but one whose girders took the form of great rectangular tubes of wrought iron through which the twin tracks ran. Since pure suspension bridges had been proved unsuitable for heavy trains, these two types of span—the plate girder and the tied arch—were to provide the essential vocabulary of bridge-builders at least until the age of mild steel.

Though the Conway bridge (which is less than 20 ft. above water-level) has since had to be provided with additional supports, Stephenson had such faith in his solution that he also adopted it at the much longer and higher bridge over the Menai Straits, which was named the Britannia bridge after a rock in mid-stream and was completed in the same year of 1849. (Plate 10). With a design based on model tests, this was nearly 1,400 ft. long and divided into two approach spans of 230 ft. and two main ones of exactly twice that length weighing over 1,500 tons each, whereas the longest girder previously fabricated had been little more than 30 ft. long. These were also set 100 ft.

above tidal waters, the high clearance—which had ruled out Stephenson's first plan for a structure of cast iron arches—being inposed by the Admiralty to allow the passage of tall-masted sailing craft. At first, however, Stephenson's advisers thought that suspension cables too would be needed to support the girders, and so he built three plain but graceful tapering towers through which to reave them—on the principle, as David Walters has expressed it, of wearing braces as well as a belt.

The cables were omitted from the final design of the Britannia bridge; but the towers with their windowed structures on top remained, and still form part of this massive and inevitable landmark. (It is typical of the smallness of our present age that the tradition of keeping white its two millioneth and final rivet has been abandoned to save a few shillings a year). Nothing more than a glimpse of it can be caught by the rail traveller, but a good impression is obtained from another masterpiece, Telford's rebuilt road suspension bridge which runs alongside as a similar work on the A5 Holyhead road does at Conway. Closer inspection shows the elegance of the balustrades of the approaches, which were designed by the railway architect Francis Thompson with leonine sculpture by John Thomas. (Plate 10).

In the year of the Great Exhibition, work was planned on what was to become one of I. K. Brunel's greatest memorials. This was the Royal Albert Bridge across the Tamar (itself a valley associated with early industry) which divided Devon from Cornwall at Saltash. Thanks to its curving approaches, this bridge (Plate 11) can be well viewed from a train crossing it on the surviving line to the deep west. The work, which was first conceived as a timber structure, was to run into financial as well as technical difficulties however, and was not to be opened until 1859. Even then it was, as it remains, a single-track bridge.

As at Menai the girders had to be high enough to clear shipping on the tidal waters below; and here too approach-ways led to two centrally-supported trusses, each 455 ft. long and weighing over 1,600 tons, which have now seen well over a century of service (very recently, however, they have been discreetly strengthened). These were of an unusual and perhaps rather ungainly construction, of which a remote ancestor can be recognised in the Gaunless bridge: the decking was supported partly by a flattened arch whose main member was a wrought-iron tube of elliptical section, and partly by suspension cables salvaged from another Brunel project which had itself run into financial difficulties. When this last—the Clifton road bridge outside Bristol—was eventually completed, it was again with secondhand Brunel chains, this time from the Hungerford bridge in London.

An even more flatly-arched tube had earlier been used by Brunel in another railway bridge, that of 1852 spanning the Wye at Chepstow, Mon. This, indeed, stood in a 'little sister' relation to the Royal Albert rather as Conway does to the Britannia. But unfortunately it had to be almost completely rebuilt a decade ago, and only the three iron piers of the original now remain.

Detailed descriptions survive of the building of the cofferdam for the cast-iron central pier at Saltash, of the pioneering use of compressed air in its caisson, and of the prefabricated trusses being floated into position (a technique which Brunel had learned by watching Stephenson's work at Menai) prior to being jacked-up 100 ft. as the masonry rose. A note of human drama is added to the story of the Royal Albert by the fact that on its opening day in May, 1859, the engineer whose name is still incised on its towers was a desperately sick man as a result of the setbacks suffered by his last and greatest ship, and that his only sight of the completed structure was taken from the railway flat-car which was almost literally Isambard Kingdon Brunel's deathbed.

For some fifteen years after 1860 few major works of conventional railway engineering were opened, possible exceptions being the Runcorn bridge across the Mersey (1863) with its 300 ft. latticed girders but rather crude decoration, and such largely 'political' cross-Thames bridges designed on the same principle—and in several cases by John Hawkshaw—as Cannon Street (1866), Grosvenor, Victoria (1867), Blackfriars (1868), and Hungerford, Charing Cross (1864), whose towers date from the Brunel passenger suspension bridge of twenty years before. Less noted but perhaps more elegant is the arched iron bridge which carries the West London line near Battersea (1863).

John Fowler's extremely elegant and forward-looking arch of Coalbrookdale cast iron across the Severn near Buildwas is, however, unique; and it is unfortunate that this, the Albert Edward Bridge of 1863 which parallels the historic road bridge built almost exactly a century before, is now open only to freight traffic. Yet perhaps the period is most vividly recreated by the cut-and-cover lines of the London underground system which were opened from 1863 onwards.

The oldest section of these, as a plaque outside Baker Street station records, is that between Paddington and Farringdon Street. Euston Square station well displays the spacious vault and ventilation shafts desirable in underground stations served by steam; indeed, sulphur can still be tasted in its air. But the engineering methods of more than a century ago can perhaps best be studied a little further east in the Moorgate area. Rather than return to the subject of underground design in the next chapter, it may also be mentioned here that features of original 'Met.' and 'District' architecture are common throughout the capital—for instance, at Gloucester Road—though despite the characteristic (and later) use of terracotta facings the system never achieved the corporate style of the Paris *Metro*. The 4 ft-gauge Glasgow underground system, which remained cable-hauled until 1935, also preserves much of its original atmosphere of 1897. And Greathead and Barlow's Thames subway at the Tower—opened in 1870 as the first to be dug with a shield of the style still visible by arrangement with the LTB at Moorgate (Northern Line) station and today marked by its decorative pavilions—can perhaps be counted as a railway relic since it was originally served by a narrow-gauge cable-car.

In a different category is another Thames tunnel, that at Wapping, whose building had engaged both Brunels (themselves following Trevithick) between 1824 and 1843; for in 1869 this was incorporated into the underground system. According to L. T. C. Rolt—who has written of the ghosts which haunt this pioneering bore—the spiral staircase at Wapping is the original one. And even on London's deep-level tubes proper, which began with the opening of the sub-Thames line between King William Street and Stockwell in 1890 (the northern part, now disused, can be visited by special arrangement), a good deal of detail in the form of fretted initials, tiling and even lampshades has survived, particularly in those twilight regions served by emergency staircases.

Returning to the main lines, Britain's next exceptional bridge is also associated with death—but not, this time, the death of one man only. For the first of the two new structures needed in the final major phase of the railway age, the straightening of routes up the indented east coast of Scotland, was that over the Tay—which, at over two miles, is still the longest bridge in Britain. It was opened in 1878; and in the next year, thanks to bad design, worse construction and almost no inspection, its thirteen central girders were swept away with the loss of 75 lives.

The present rather undistinguished replacement by W. H. Barlow and his son was opened alongside the line of the old in 1887 (Plate 13). This was still a wrought-iron girder structure—perhaps the last important one in the world, for British regulations insisted on the use of this material long after Bessemer's and even Siemens' inventions had proved their qualities. It indeed incorporated a good deal of material from its predecessor. And these lattice girders, together with the approach lines and the standing piers, must serve as another of the few examples included in this book of the dozens of sites associated with classic railway accidents.

Three years after the new Tay bridge, Baker and Fowler's three-piered and cantilevered structure across the Forth was opened. With its spans of over 1700 ft. standing 150 ft. above the estuary and its claim to be the world's first major mild-steel bridge, this impressive but ungainly structure whose form is engraved on the national mind as an epitome of the last, heavy years of the century finally closed the classic age of British railway building (Plate 13). It is interesting to note that only in very recent years have the Forth, Tay and Saltash spans been duplicated by road bridges.

For, though the now-disused bowstring arch over the Tyne at West Wylam (Plate 12) was then new and the Connel Ferry cantilevers and some good inland structures such as that embellished with the arms of the North Staffordshire Railway at Longton were still to come, larger and more original bridges were being planned overseas as the Victorian age neared its end.

Even on the Forth itself (where the over-confident Bouch would have built a death-trap of a suspension bridge had not his disgrace intervened before more was erected than a tower on Inch Garvie), a French specialist had been called in to advise on the caissons; and when the bridge came to be opened it was by the future Edward VII and not the queen. But it was only 50 years since Robert Stephenson had completed the first trunk line, 75 since his father's experiments with locomotive traction, and 100 since wooden rails were still *de rigueur* and the ideal of a national network of railways unborn. And today, as another century moves towards its close, perhaps even 1890 can be regarded as a date of antiquity.

Furthermore, one final prototype structure remains to be added as a codicil to this chapter. Fittingly it is to be found on one of the last lines to be opened, the West Highland railway's extension to Mallaig, Scotland; for where this spanned the head of Loch Shiel at Glenfinnan in Inverness a curved and 21-arched viaduct was completed in 1898 was the first of its kind in the kingdom to be built in concrete. There were also some concrete bridges on the line. This material, however, was used only through the shortage of local alternatives and was assembled in the 'mass' or non-reinforced type of construction—for which concrete is not well adapted—into a bridge still essentially of Stephensonian form.

It was hence the material, and not the design, which was new—and then only to Britain. But the date of the opening of this lovely line (still, if dubiously, open to passenger traffic) at the end of an heroic century marks a fitting transition towards the present from a tradition of bridge-building which the railwaymen has inherited from the tramwaymen—and they themselves from a line of descent at least 4,000 years older. For even the Causey arch is young by comparison with the bridges of Rome, let alone Mesopotamia.

Many elegant and curious bridges have been passed over in this chapter, and little mention has been made in it of either swing bridges (which are mechanical rather than structural feats, though it may be mentioned here that the first such was opened at Trowse, Norfolk, in 1848) or major works of which only slight traces subsist. Typical of the latter is the Solway bridge, which like its 4,000 ft. sister (once England's longest) at Sharpness on the Severn was damaged by act of God when its traffic usefulness was in any case coming to an end and was hence not rebuilt. In a rather different category, the great inland viaduct of Crumlin, Mon—opened in 1862 and showing the first thoughtful use of lattice construction in its wrought-iron girders supported by cast-iron columns—was deliberately dismantled a few years ago and whilst still in fine condition, to save about £2,500 in annual upkeep. For a sum equivalent to the salary of some Assistant Regional Secretary to a Committee on Local Culture, Wales lost for ever the only structure of any dignity in the Ebbw Vale and Britain a monument of great technical importance.

Even higher than Crumlin was the featherweight viaduct of 1859 built some 1350 ft. above sea level at Glen Belah in the moorlands outside Kirkby Stephen. But this little-known yet graceful structure, which was erected in a mere four months yet which probably represented at the time of its destruction not only the most ambitious use of cast iron piers surviving in the world but a unique example of Bow's flexibly-pinned structures, was dismantled and sold for scrap (together with its slightly smaller but otherwise identical sister at Deepdale) after the closure of its line a decade ago. It is hard to imagine such vandalism being committed on Eiffel's comparable bridges in southern France.

So Britain's two loftiest viaducts (for at both Crumlin and Glen Belah the roadbed was some 200 ft. above the valley floor) perished save for their abutments, and proved how secretively Britain has been robbed of such national treasures as involve maintenance costs and have a scrap value. Another such loss has been that of the Meldon viaduct of 1874 near Okehampton, Devon. But a fair number of smaller yet still notable bridgeworks remain. In the first fifty years of the railway age, for instance, single-span cast-iron arches—often with interesting embellishments—were erected in such situations as the crossing of an embanked line over a city street.

Modern traffic-weight restrictions have compelled the replacement of many of these and the encasing of others in concrete; but enough remain to make the survivors far from rarities, though still worthy of attention. Good examples are to be found in Manchester, near Rugby, on the Dulwich College estate (1862, by the younger Charles Barry), in the arches of 1850 which carry the up lines of the former Great Northern railway over the Nene at Peterborough, and (a magnificent example of decorative foundry-work, due again to the GNR and dating from 1878) at Friargate, Derby (Plate 14).

Other and more purely decorative cast-iron work, including such blazons of the arms of the pre-amalgamation companies as were recently stripped from Charing Cross, London, but remain on Blackfriars bridge (Plate 14), and more horticultural embellishments too, can of course be found on structures in themselves unremarkable. (Thus, Cannon Street bridge today is less than beautiful: but it still bears much of the 1,100 tons of ornamental metal with which it was laden in deference to its proximity to St Paul's.) Nor should one overlook many humble brick bridges, particularly those built on the skew: unattractive as their purple 'engineer's brick' may be, their craftsmanship marks one of the last stages of development of an art brought to Britain from the Low Countries in medieval times—an art which also flowered in the building of the retaining walls and buttresses of cuttings.

Timber bridges never became really popular in Britain, though most systems had at least one example of the use of this cheap but usually short-lived material. The York museum, for instance, preserves a laminated member from a bridge which survived at North Shields for nearly a century, mainly because no trains ever ran over it; and a wooden lift bridge which remained in use until recently is in store at Leicester. Wood was, however, favoured by Brunel (the last of whose series of timber viaducts in the deep West, whose piers can still be seen (Plate 13), survived until 1934, because of his mistrust of cast iron) and was also used on the coastal stretch of the Cambrian railway opened in 1867.

The future of this line is currently in doubt. But for the moment timber construction is still represented, if more massively than elegantly, by Thomas Savin's 800 ft. estuarine viaduct (whose swing-opening span of iron was replaced in 1899) over the Mawddach at Barmouth (Plate 13) and by the Afon Dwyryd bridge at Penrhyndeudraeth further north. This latter also carries a toll roadway, and so may prove the last timber survivor of them all.

## *VI STATIONS AND THEIR ARCHITECTURE*

THAT the Liverpool and Manchester is recognised as the world's first indisputable railway is largely due to the fact that from its opening it had, if almost accidentally, used locomotives for passenger haulage. It is hence fitting that there have survived from this line representatives not only of its civil engineering works (such as have been described in the last chapter) and its motive power (such as will be mentioned in the next), but of its provisions for handling passengers too. At the Liverpool end the original Crown Street station was short-lived and even the temporary, timber beginnings of today's Lime Street complex have been engulfed. But Manchester has been more fortunate in that a substantial part of John Foster's unusually ambitious and truss-roofed original station in Liverpool Road, including the rail level 'platforms', has survived.

This building, which also houses a few special exhibits such as a section of stone-sleepered track and the station bell and which is faced by a fine contemporaneous warehouse is now used as a freight depot; and as in most such cases those with a serious interest in railway history are shown round by advance arrangement or (with a little luck) by arriving when a suitably senior member of the staff is available. It merits a pilgrimage if only for contrast with the Stockton 'station'; for this is beyond doubt much the oldest structure in the world to be built with an eye to the convenience of travellers by rail. But it must be regretted that the equally interesting terminus of the line from Leeds, opened in 1838, has suddenly been demolished.

Immense as the engineering achievements of the late 1830s and early 1840s were, it has already been noted that they derived directly from the techniques of the canal and tramway engineers. With passenger stations, however, the pioneer railwaymen had to design from the ground up. They were not professional architects, and they usually employed these only on major projects. But their problems were largely without precedent, for two main types of structure—the town terminal and the village station—seemed to be needed, and in neither case did either the inn-yards of the stage-routes or the canal companies' wharfs provide a suitable model. Furthermore, the smaller stations had to be multiplied in the form of subtle variations on a basic plan.

It has often been noted as remarkable that the Stephensons, father and son, should have made such great contributions to both civil and mechanical engineering. (The same, though, is true of the Rennies, Rastrick, Brunel and other contemporaries). In addition, of course, George pioneered industrial logistics as well as inventing such useful devices as the miner's lamp and the straight cucumber. Robert's unconvenanted gift to the common good was that—usually aided only by his own assistants and local masons, and working at the end of Britain's greatest age of domestic design and the beginning of a half-century-long conflict of styles—he supervised the design of whole series of rural stations. These not only admirably served their functions but were well attuned to local vernaculars even when found as far afield as Normandy—a fact which helped the social acceptance of the railway in country and suburban areas, and which means that even today the stations of Britain can remain a delicate indicator of regional and geological frontiers.

Many of the smaller stations of the 1830s have outlived the lines and communities which they served, some being now adapted as farm cottages or for more eccentric purposes such as boathouses, boys' clubs or Greek Orthodox chapels and others standing shuttered and half-decrepit to await a tenant or—with the help of the ubiquitous young vandal—to fall down. Yet others have recently been more officially wrecked: the last two examples of Brunel's smaller buildings for the Bristol line, form a shameful example here. But one sequence of a dozen little-changed Robert Stephenson stations, dating from about 1836, can still be found on the Newcastle–Carlisle railway. This has, indeed, had a less interrupted history (structurally speaking) than has most of its contemporaries.

Of its stations—'Small, stone-built and Tudor', as Nicholas Taylor describes them—'the least spoiled is at (Stephenson's) own birthplace of Wylam. Others still open include Stocksfield, Hexham, Bardon Mill . . . and Brampton Junction'. It was at the last that another railway 'first' was scored with Thomas Edmundson's invention of the traditional type of printed ticket, his original machine now being preserved at the Science Museum, London.

The termini of this formative period necessarily proved less adequate for future needs. And though a few—such as the 1840 station of the Preston railway in Penny Street, Lancaster, which is now a nurses' home—have casually survived, they have generally met one of three ends. These are to be destroyed utterly, to be incorporated as fragments of later stations, or to be demoted to goods-depot status.

In addition to two others mentioned here, for instance, a number of BR freight stations still in use such as the turreted Bricklayers' Arms in south-east London (1840) betray their origins by such features as a lack of raised platforms. (The most interesting, Nine Elms, is however now being demolished). And an example of survival by engulfment is to be found at Bristol (Temple Meads), where Brunel's structure of 1841 above the old broad-gauge terminus represents one of the earliest—and certainly one of the best—experiments in railway Gothic.

Jack Simmons has described its (admittedly largely decorative) timber hammer-beam roof, whose width of 72 ft. is greater than that of Westminster

PLATE 17

(above) The entry to Curzon Street station, Birmingham, is a now-unique example of Hardwick's work for the company. The long facade of Chester (below) Illustrates Dobson's more individual treatment of the theme a decade later.

PLATE 18

The magnificent porticos of Huddersfield (above) and Monkwearmouth (below) speak for themselves of the confidence of the early railway age.

PLATE 19

Above are two details of the renaissance school of station architecture—the loggia at Melton Mowbray (above left) and the campanile of Nuneaton (above right). Other architects looked to the same age but models nearer home, as in the cottage Tudor of Fenny Stratford (left) or Tite's baronial work at Carlisle (left below).

PLATE 20 Romantic, eclectic, unique—Scott's St Pancras, London.

PLATE 21

Noble train-shed roofs—straight by Barlow at St Pancras (above) and curved by Prosser at Newcastle Central (below).

PLATE 22

Two examples of the somewhat later 'Jacobethan' approach to station design are Shrewsbury (above) and Stoke (below).

PLATE 23
Even a dull station may be enlivened by its detail in metal, stone or wood. Examples here are the ironwork at Kettering (above), the very unusual and little-known series of eight *amoretti* performing such humble railway tasks as porterage on the tympani of Liverpool Street (left), and the valencing at Westcliff-on-Sea (left below).

PLATE 24

A miscellany of the kind of lineside features which can still—just—be discovered on Britain's railways.

Hall, as the grandest monument still surviving from the early years of the railway age. The hall is now ironically degraded to a temporary car park, and of the sister-building at Bath little of the original survives. But two other relics subsist of early railway Bristol, these being Brunel's Perpendicular office building of 1841 to the left of the forecourt (now an enquiry office) and the corresponding building of the Bristol and Exeter company—erected in 1854 in a Jacobean style and still used as a railway headquarters—to its right.

Needless to say, the whole of this historic complex surrounding M. Digby Wyatt's Tudor station of 1870 (which has itself, as is the case with most such buildings, been diminished in elegance by the passage of time and thoughtless additions) is now threatened with 'redevelopment'. Had this been carried out a century ago when a more central station was first proposed, Bristolians would at least not have to travel a mile to take their trains. But today the rebuilding of Temple Meads would be a vandalism balanced by no gain in convenience.

That vandalism is not too strong a word for the threat which hangs over so many stations of distinction is of course proved by the case of Euston, London, which perfectly exemplified that need to impress urban investors which complemented the desire to reassure rural passengers. For this building was tragic in that it passed through the phase of despoilment only to meet the final fate of demolition. Step by step for nearly a century the station had sprawled to meet operating needs, the noble propylaeum had been robbed of a pair of flanking pavilions, and the coffer-ceilinged great hall itself had come to owe as much to Lutyens as to Hardwick. But even at the opening of the 1950s BR regarded the Euston shareholders' room with pride and the station was given a costly face-lift.

Now all is gone, except for Stephenson's statue and two pavilions added in 1870; and though this book is not concerned with vanished glories it must add its protest at the loss of the unique hall and of the granite Doric arch which stood as not only a gateway to the north but a symbol of all the forward-looking enterprise of the early railways. Rightly, the future of this national monument (and whatever its absolute aesthetic value it was, on historical grounds alone, a thousand times more worthy of preservation than the Marble Arch which was *not* moved to make way for cars) was referred to the Cabinet. Wrongly, it was abandoned at the demands of a badly-planned tube line and ended as a pile of rubble—on which, it was reported, the later-added and gilded letters EUSTON could still be descried—in a mason's yard.

Possibly fragments can still be found by souvenir-hunters out Edgware way, for the breakers have not yet managed to dispose of the corpse of London's only comparable monument, Rennie's old Waterloo bridge. Certainly the nation should have saved the whole. But as it was, this 'Roman work, conceived in the Roman spirit and accomplished with Roman perseverance' met a Roman end, and was destroyed by barbarians.

A memorial of the Euston of long pre-electric days can, however, still be found at Camden Town. The steep climb out of the terminus to clear the

Regent's canal and the low power of early locomotives implied that (as at Liverpool) trains had to be cable-hauled over the first mile or so, and accordingly, Stephenson's classically-detailed engine-shed of 1837 was sited at the head of this incline. As with a number of later such sheds, some of which are still in use in the diesel age, this was built on a circular plan with a central turntable. After later methods of working had made it an embarassment it became a gin repository, and the 'round house' has now emerged in the even odder guise of a proleterian playhouse. Those who wish to soften the effects of an evening of class-war with reflections in suitable surroundings as to what the industrial revolution was really all about should contact "Centre 42", London.

At the far end of the same line, Birmingham (Curzon Street) still preserves its facade (Plate 17), though the buildings which included the first railway refreshment room have recently vanished together with the Grand Junction terminus and the warehouse where the inaugural banquet was held. Even this frontage is fortunate to have survived so far; and it certainly needs a watchful eye kept on it, if only because Birmingham is in need of its antiquities. But for the moment Philip Hardwick's smaller and Ionic counterpart of 1838 to his vanished Euston arch still stands. And though in a somewhat dilapidated condition and decidedly grim surroundings, it expresses what Christian Barman has heavily termed the hieratic as opposed to the social or functional projection of the railways' image.

The humbleness of the accommodation behind this facade would seem to give some substance to Pugin's and Ruskin's strictures to the effect that such early stations were too rich in impressive monuments and too poor in decent facilities for trains and their passengers. But it may be that, if only subconsciously, their engineers sensed that the problems of terminal working would be solved only by trial and error and that it would be wise to wait a decade or so before indulging in anything more costly and permanent than iron or timber shedding. Meanwhile, though, a few grand gestures were called for.

Typical of the difficulties of early railway operation was the fact that, once passengers had overcome their first feelings of awe at the steam locomotive, they tended to wander across the tracks as casually as if these were the cobbles of an inn yard. This carelessness led to travellers being kept under the strict surveillance to be found today in Spanish railway stations and in airports everywhere. It was partly to simplify their shepherding that, wherever possible, departures were handled from a single flanking track and arrivals at another, with up to a dozen central lines being used only for shunting and (a significant term) stabling. In particular, the 'keep left' rule of running led to departure facilities such as booking offices and refreshment rooms being grouped at the centre of Platform 1—an arrangement which persists in the earlier U-shaped terminals of London and other cities, unsuited as it is to present needs.

One early 'forebuilding', however, was delightfully successful as both an architectural composition and a working arrangement. This was the Italianate Brighton which—though marred by accretions on the town side—

still stands substantially as it did when opened in 1841. The touch of its brilliant designer David Mocatta—a pupil of John Soane, and perhaps the first man consciously to adopt a modular or 'unit' plan for a series of buildings—can also, of course, be recognised on the engineering works referred to in the previous chapter. Lewis Cubitt's Dover Town, built two years later and described by Christian Barman as 'gay and dashing' though it also has an ecclesiastical presence, is in the same style but rendered unique by its massive tower; and a few fragments of what was once Scotland's finest station at Glasgow (Queen St: 1842) may possibly survive the current works.

At large through-stations—and in particular Great Western ones such as Reading—another device for keeping passengers under control was resorted to. This was the routing of traffic in both directions alongside a single platform, a plan which saved leg-work for public and staff at the cost of some inconvenience in train working. Today, only the arcaded Cambridge (built in 1845 by Sancton Wood, who is also credited with some elegant small stations on this line, such as Great Chesterfield) retains such a layout, though there it proved so satisfactory in handling denser and more complex traffic than now uses the station that it is hard to see that anyone would benefit by its being rebuilt on conventional lines. But the unique status of Cambridge is not due to any donnish quiddity, but is rather a residue of a plan once not uncommon.

Of the greater stations built in this age, Lewis Cubitt's Kings Cross of 1852 stands virtually in a class of its own. Alone of London's earlier termini it has survived almost in its virgin state; and even the unusually high plat-derived from the low track-level imposed by the Regent's canal tunnel set it apart from its peers. Its plain internal arrangements also include a departure centre on the 'side of No. 1 platform' plan.

The relegation of suburban traffic to an annexe has also added to an air of lofty isolation and concentration on the sleeping car trade. Unfortunately one cannot take seriously BR's claim that the building will be unspoiled by the new wing of yet more railway offices (the existing ones along the arrival side are, of course, by Cubitt) planned to rise in front of it. This will, however, probably prove little worse as a concealer of the basement than the canopied cab-shed which preceded it.

For the past few years, in fact—and thanks mainly to the underground workings which have cleared the forecourt—London has had a rare opportunity to admire Cubitt's buttressed facade. Much has been written in favour of this wall of stock bricks which has been sympathetically treated by BR, and most of it is deserved praise. For the twin arches certainly elegantly define the come-and-go function of the train shed behind them; and though the tower which houses a clock (acquired at second-hand from the Great Exhibition) is too small by half it not only punctuates the composition and forms a link with the symmetrical bell-cotes of early nineteenth-century stables and canal buildings but also points out that railways should set a standard of timekeeping.

The station is still flanked by a hotel built by the same architect. This curved building is of no special note in itself, and furthermore is set well to the side of the station—as is the oldest survivor of its kind, Francis Thompson's finely-proportioned Derby of 1840. After the railways began to enter seriously into the catering trade in the 1860s, though, the usual plan was to let the hotel form the fore building of the station itself. This it did in Hardwick's renaissance extension to Paddington which is still discernible under a jazz-age reshaping, and in the rather attractive Frenchified confection of Charing Cross which was built by the son of the designer of the Houses of Parliament, E. M. Barry, in 1864. The same architect's fine Cannon Street buildings have now been completely demolished.

To consider station hotels in detail would take this book outside its terms of reference. But the Victorian companies did much to shape not only hotel architecture but hotel life in the age of which a ghost still haunts not only Gleneagles but many caravanserai which BR no longer manage. And so this chapter should make at least passing reference not only to such prestigious buildings but to the more provincial and Jacobethan approach of such companies as the North Staffordshire railway at Stoke (Plate 22) and Stone (1848)—the whole centre of Stoke being laid out by that company.

Of the other major stations built in an age when proportion if not ornament still followed eighteenth-century canons and when design remained, in John Betjeman's words, 'stately but not sumptuous, spreading but not soaring', Wyatt's Paddington remembers its first state of being simply an open, arcaded forecourt to the tracks only by its side-entrance and the name of 'The Lawn'. It is today mainly notable for its train-shed, a fairly early (1854) example of a feature referred to later and one which, since the loss of the Coal Exchange, perhaps represents London's finest work in cast iron.

In the case of Paddington the semi-elliptical roof is unusually complex though visually homogeneous, being not only multi-aisled (with spans of up to 100 ft.) but crossed by transepts which originally gave head-room to carriage traversers and still further varied by a much later cone-shaped extension, bearing the GWR arms, over the cab-road. The best viewpoint is from behind one of the balconies of the office block on the west side: business or self-confidence gains admission to the corridor behind these, and enables one to escape the clutter of BR passenger 'amenities' which seem particularly incongruous at Paddington. The *flamboyant* mouldings interestingly foreshadow some later *art nouveau* motif.

Of the final example of London's early-Victorian terminals, London Bridge, it is perhaps kindest to say only that it was begun in 1838 and has not yet been completed. Some pleasant Italianate features however—and particularly the tower—lend it a little distinction.

Though they epitomise parallel developments in other great cities, the railheads of London form a subject in themselves; and so this chapter must return to the main stream of development. In the 1840s this was flowing fast, for the station builders had moved on from the near-miraculous accident to more conscious architectural principles. Nothing illustrates this fact more clearly than the work of Francis Thompson, a Derby architect already referred to who combined elements of Hardwick's grandeur and Mocatta's delicacy in stations which ruled local vernaculars into a classic symmetry and who, as early as 1842, appears to have published a portfolio entitled 'Railway Architecture'.

Thompson's stations divide into two groups, of which the earlier were built (mainly in local stone) before 1840 for George Stephenson's North Midland line from Derby to Sheffield. None is now in use, but the original Ambergate—which should not be confused with the elegant, gabled fragment of the later deltoid junction to the north—still largely survives. So, too, does the perfect Wingfield, described by Barman as 'an example in the strict classical manner that is unequalled anywhere' but today boarded-up and closed to traffic.

A later Derbyshire station of some note is Buxton, where in 1863 the house-proud local authorities insisted that the rival companies seeking access to the spa should agree on a joint composition. In fact the twin stations, though almost identical, had interesting differences of detail, which can hardly be studied now since one has recently been demolished and the other appears to be crumbling away. Other stations of interest on this line are the abandoned terminus of Rowsley (for Chatsworth) which is by Joseph Paxton, and the later buildings at Cromford and Matlock Bath with which the architect of the Crystal Palace may also have been associated. Only the now-derelict LNWR terminus at Oxford, though, took over the modular components designed for that historic building.

Francis Thompson's own second group of stations (which showed a more pronounced family likeness that did the North Midland ones) were built for Robert Stephenson's extension of the LNWR through North Wales to Holyhead nearly a decade later. The elegant main block of Holywell (Flint) still stands, as does Flint itself—'a landmark in an undistinguished town', as David Lloyd notes—and Conway where even Thompson was forced into pure Gothic. Of his larger stations at Bangor and Chester the former has been smothered in additions; and the latter (in which the architect corrected some mistakes he had made at Derby) is a typical example of those buildings which appear magnificent in contemporary lithographs when imaginatively surrounded by cows and peasants but which nowadays—though unchanged save for the inevitable canopy on the town side—go almost unnoticed (Plate 17). Still, it is a striking facade to have emerged from the committee-work of five independent companies.

By the later 1840s railway architecture had become eclectic. But despite experiments in such exotic styles as that represented by the splendid and unique—but anonymous and abandoned—baroque 'orangery' of 1848 at Newmarket, Suffolk (an affluent town in an area not given to architectural extravagance), there were accepted norms. For smaller stations the choice was between Tudor as in William Tite's royal Windsor (Riverside), Berks., of 1850 and William Tress's attractive Battle, Sussex—a place, as Michael Robbins has commented, which the Victorians thought to be particularly mediaeval—of 1852, and a more urbane Italianate often elaborated with most un-Italian drip-mouldings. Mocatta had indeed made this latter so successful that it was becoming known as the 'railway style' and imitated in *cottages ornés* and the villas of new suburbs.

In some cases the campanili served a practical end, though of Brunel's pretty 'atmospheric' stations along the North Devon coast only Starcross (1846) and part of Dawlish survive. (The timber-faced Torre, probably also by Brunel, was built two years later.) But everywhere the design of cantilevered platform verandas became almost the last folk-art, for their pelmets are almost as diverse as are English stations themselves: one of the best displays is to be seen at Kettering, Northants (Plate 23). More surprisingly, work in cast iron such as is well illustrated at Great Malvern, Worcs., shows as wide a variety.

At least one large station built in a pure Tudor idiom survives, though in an extended form: this is the towered Carlisle (Citadel) of 1847, which was later to be used by nine companies and is described by Barman—who particularly praises the attention given to the generally-disregarded buildings on the island platform—as Britain's 'finest piece of railway architecture in the sixteenth-century collegiate style'. The architect here was again the prolific Tite (Plate 19). But for city termini and semi-termini a classical order—usually more Grecian than Roman—was generally favoured, serious Gothic being as yet rare and even such hybrids as appeared at Shrewsbury (Plate 22—built 'in the best romantic tradition', as an account put it) not very common. Fortunately a number of examples of these noble buildings have survived to be appreciated even by BR. And the finest of them all is undoubtedly John Dobson's Newcastle (Central) of 1850 (Plate 21).

Even as it stands, the great portico which originally gave access to a single platform is fully worthy of a city not poor in buildings of the classical revival. But through a curious chapter in railway history this was in fact added by another hand some two decades later, and the architect's original design—which he was ordered to alter during construction so as to make better use of the space—would have resulted in one of the great buildings of the world. Dobson himself, a Newcastle man, has indeed been described as the finest of all railway architects. Earlier stations of his include London Road, Carlisle—now a freight depot, and suggesting that he may have advised Robert Stephenson over other stations on that line—and the noteworthy Gateshead (1841); and he also collaborated with Stephenson on several bridges in the far north of England.

But the most important of Dobson's achievements was an engineering one in the sense that he was the first to devise long wrought-iron ribs rolled to a designed curve. These, used in place of the previous short and straight sections or the wood employed in such early glazed roofs as Brunel's Exeter (St Thomas) of 1846, made possible the true 'train sheds'—those bold, overall arched spans of iron and glass so characteristic of the greater British station and today so alarmingly expensive in upkeep. These became increasingly common after Paxton's *tour de force* for the Great Exhibition of 1851. But Dobson's three magnificent spans at Newcastle, each of 55 ft. and built on a curve of fairly short radius, were the first in the world.

Second in splendour as a classical station is Huddersfield (Plate 18), by J. P. Pritchett (1847). This too was originally single-platformed; and though its fine frontage has been spoiled by later accretions it has at least not been hemmed-in. The grand facades of G. T. Andrews' Hull (surnamed Paragon, 1848) and Dobson's Monkwearmouth, Co. Durham, of the same year (Plate 18: this station, which appears to have been built so impressively to handle so little traffic in commemoration of the election to parliament of the railway king, George Hudson, is now closed and hence threatened) also follow the classic orders, as does the charming but disused Ashby-de-la-Zouch. Stations which use them on a smaller scale and with more freedom include the elegant Scarborough (1845), Ely (1846), Warwick (Milverton: 1844), Cheltenham (Lansdown), whose Doric columns of 1840 have already been destroyed and which is now endangered by total reconstruction, and perhaps Fenchurch Street, London (mainly 1853). The unspoiled Bath (Green Park, 1870, now also closed and threatened) is the last purely classic station.

Yet, at the same time as these were arising, the little stations which have fittingly been compared to the lodges of great estates continued to add their characteristic punctuation marks to the landscape. In East Anglia alone, for instance, attractive stations still in use include Stamford, Gainsborough, Louth and Spalding in Lincolnshire, Audley End in Essex and Littleport in Cambridgeshire, the gabled Swaffham in Norfolk, and in Suffolk Stowmarket, the domed Bury St Edmunds, and Thurston. Several of the best of these are by Frederick Barnes of Ipswich, who also designed the now-closed station of Needham Market.

Another interesting group—most of the members of which, though divisible into several sub-classes, share a family likeness—is to be found on the old North Staffordshire system. Typical trademarks of the Potteries are groove-tiled platform edgings and the 'knot' badge, as is visible at Keele. The best series was to be found in the Churnet valley; and though many of its members (such as Trentham) have been demolished, certain station houses still stand as at Alton.

Bedford (Midland Road), if not of great beauty, is noteworthy as an example of its period—1859—which has survived virtually unaltered. And a further miscellany of small stations which have been commended would range from Llandilo in Carmarthen and Wemyss Bay in Renfrewshire to Wateringbury in Kent, a typical example of the 'country house' school of design. It would include Frome (Som) with its wooden roof and length of early 'Barlow' track in the yard, the Fisherton section of Salisbury, Atherstone and Hampton-in-Arden (Warwick), a South-Western series—largely by Tite—including Southampton Terminus, Micheldever and Gosport, Gobowen, Acklington (Nthbd), Earlestown (Lancs), Burton-on-Trent, Tynemouth, Leatherhead, Sandon (Staffs), Fenny Stratford (Plate 19) and Woburn Sands (Beds)—a remarkably cosy structure though also ducal, this, with its half-timbering and barge-board gables—and the larger Hereford. Castle Howard, Richmond and Pocklington in Yorkshire, the gabled Northampton (Bridge Street), Thrapston (Northants) are now closed.

Perhaps London's best small relic is the station house at Kilburn High Road; but Barnes Common, Crystal Palace (low level) and Greenwich (1838) are also worthy of note.

Yet is would also, unfortunately, be easy to make as long a list of small stations of individuality and charm—if not, perhaps, great architectural importance—which have been lost in the past few years. The series of Italian-Gothic stations on the North London line, for instance, has now been largely supplanted by prefabricated 'bus stops' except for Camden Road and Broad Street itself: the latter, which has recently lost its roof, is a station of 1866 by W. Baker where the adjoining goods depot in Eldon Street (which is now partly used as a car park and contains some interesting hydraulic machinery) is also worth attention. In several such cases the pattern of Euston has been followed on a smaller scale and without publicity, the present age disposing of buildings whose proportions had earlier been marred by late-Victorian enlargements.

More than one critic has suggested that the great age of station-building ended with the second slump in railway construction in the mid-1850s, and that good design did not begin to revive for more than thirty years thereafter. Certainly a first direct thrust spent itself shortly after the mid-point of the century in a battle of styles as academic Gothic began to assert itself. But stations of interest continued to be built well after the quarter-century point of the railway age.

Probably the most distinguished of these is York—that slightly-bombed 'gentleman among stations' as a Victorian commentator called it, of 1877 with its vast and mysterious curving roof. This iron forest designed by Thomas Prosser who took over Dobson's work at Newcastle, forms part of what was in its time the largest such complex in the world. The accompanying hotel, with some good ironwork within, is of the same period. The whole replaced the earlier (1851) Italianate station by G. T. Andrews within the walls—and approached by rail *via* a Gothic arch pierced through them—of which outbuildings now house the regional museum and the main block represents the earliest hotel integrated with a station.

But one should not forget the corporate contribution to the national scene made by the dozens of decent, quasi-Palladian, stock-brick suburban stations built by the south-of-the-Thames companies in the 1860s. Just a century later, these have begun to be systematically replaced by decent, prefabricated, steel-and-concrete variations on the same theme. Nobody could make out a strong case for the preservation of any individual building of the quality of, say, Sevenoaks; but with their associated offices these formed part of a scene peculiar to a certain way of life at a certain period. It is true that at the present rate it would take several hundred years for Britain's 3,000-odd surviving stations to be rebuilt. But before it is too late one such complex, at least, should have its face lifted and be scheduled—if scheduling, from which national property is in any case ironically exempted, can serve any purpose in an age of thoughtless rapacity—for preservation through too-fast-moving times. This would be small reward for a century of service.

For railway architecture does not concern stations alone, though they form its archetype to such a degree that this chapter can perhaps be excused for having concentrated on them. (It is noteworthy there are several published books devoted to station architecture whilst there has never been even a paper on the stylistic content of bridges and tunnel-portals, and that only in one page at the end of a monograph on railway architecture does Barman refer to the type of structure described in the previous chapter.) Furthermore, between the works of civil engineering and the stations to which attention has rightly been paid as a witness of early Victorian taste and craftsmanship, there are a host of other railway 'fixed assets' worthy of attention and, perhaps, preservation.

The station pub; the station-master's and porter's houses which often outlast the station itself, and the crossing-keeper's cottage: the warehouses which were built as worthy descendants of those of the canal age as late as 1865 (Dulcie St, Manchester) or even the 1880s (Huddersfield): the early office buildings such as survive from the East Lancashire railway in Bolton Street, Bury: the characteristic seaside or pleasure architecture of railway ferry shelters at, for instance, Harwich and of such oddities as cliff lifts (e.g. Hastings and even Bridgnorth): the signal-boxes of the fifties and sixties with their differences between companies (high-pedestalled on the LNWR, richly ornamented on the Great Northern): even such details as water-towers (that at Blisworth, the only survivor from the pioneer lines of the 1830s, has recently been destroyed—and how long will any such remain standing now that they have outlived their purpose?): all these are part of the English scene and are in danger of vanishing from it. As with run-of-the-line stations, it would be hard to justify preservation in every individual case; but whole species must not be allowed to vanish. A station like Tunbridge Wells (Central) is *only* a station like Tunbridge Wells (Central), just as a blue whale is *only* a blue whale, until its kind are in danger of extinction.

Nor should the 'railway towns' be overlooked here, though this term unfortunately covers two different concepts. Of the random manufacturing cities created or vastly stimulated by the railways only the very earliest such as Middlesbrough have interest or merit, and even then they do not possess it to a very noticeable degree. Except perhaps in the extreme north of England the lines arrived just at the end of a period of consistently good architecture, so that the railway station itself is commonly the best building in industrial cities unfortunate enough not to have benefited from the canal age. But in a different category are the communities planned by the railway companies themselves and often for their own purposes.

Even in this sense the phrase 'railway town' has a pejorative meaning acquired from the late-Victorian, red-brick spread of Crewe. But a belt south of the tracks at Swindon, comprising artisans' cottages of 1843, a few communal buildings, and Gilbert Scott's fine church of St Mark (the dedication, surely, being suggested as an act of filial piety by the younger Brunel) forms an admirable estate. The rather charming resort of Saltburn, Yorks, was developed in the 1860s by the Stockton and Darlington company, whose line ran right into its main hotel. And even towards the end of the century individual schemes were built—such as the Lancashire and Yorkshire railway's works at Horwich in 1886—which were models of functional convenience if not of elegance, whilst the North Eastern's offices outside Darlington (1912) are at least striking.

But it is still the station which, for the casual traveller in particular, represents railway architecture; and so this chapter should end with mention of a last such building. It is a London terminus; but it is not Marylebone, though the Grecian plasterwork of the hotel which now forms BR's headquarters, and has hence been sympathetically treated by them, stands in contrast to the humble vernacular of other Great Central buildings and the station bar is charming. It is not one of the south-of-the-Thames companies' later properties; for despite Victoria's mosaic mural map only Blackfriars (1886) is notable, and then mainly for that portico with its suggestion of *wagons-lits* about to depart for all stations to St Petersburg. It is not even Liverpool Street (1874) with its gothic train-shed roof and delightful series of bas-relief industrial cupidons (Plate 23). It is, of course, the complex begun when the Midland railway acquired its own terminus in the capital in 1868, St Pancras. (Plate 20)

Little over three decades had passed since the erection of the Euston arch. But few pairs of structures could be more disparate in feeling than Hardwick's simple and confident statement of power and Gilbert Scott's romantic blend of almost every age (and four national traditions) of Gothic which owes much but not all to his earlier design for the Foreign Office. Behind the building completed in 1876, however, stands Barlow's single-span train shed finished eight years earlier, with its height of 100 ft., its coverage of nearly 170,000 square feet, the name of the Butterley company proudly cast on its every third column, and its buried tie-beams—very slightly dated, perhaps, even a century ago, yet despite Barlow's curious belief that a ridged arch would reduce wind-resistance an even more notable example of engineer's architecture than its neighbour at King's Cross. (Plate 21)

These two sections—the fore-buildings with their hotel which is currently used as still further railway offices, and the train shed itself which is mirrored at Manchester Central—derive from different traditions, a fact which should particularly be borne in mind since the future of the station is in some uncertainty. 'I have no doubt,' wrote John Betjeman some twenty years ago, 'that British Railways will do away with St Pancras altogether . . . It is too beautiful and romantic to survive. It is not of this age.' Very recently, BR indeed announced that they regarded the station as redundant, with the result that the air was filled with schemes for its future ranging from its re-instatement as a hotel to its conversion to a sports centre or, more sensibly, transport museum.

Since then, however, there has been another of those reversals of policy which have marked the period of nationalisation, and for the present, the hotel will remain an office-block. Though it was ridiculed even in its own age, it is an immensely picturesque and ingenious building which overseas visitors have been seen to enter with prayer-book in hand, and it has become a landmark whose, "terrific Gothic"—as Hamilton Ellis has written—soars into the 'patient London sky'. Internally (and, as in most such cases, a purposeful look should gain admission) there is a good deal of curious detail. But the outstanding feature is the great staircase, which aims at a target of around the year 1500 but is graced by a tableau from the Romaunt of the Rose. What connection this idyll had with the Midland railway is obscure, but one can hope that the present officials—some of whom actually *live* in the attics of this fantastic Xanadu—gain inspiration from it. A glance at Somers Town goods station (and potato market) alongside, a contemporary and now somewhat moth-eaten building by Scott whose graduated brick-work Betjeman has described as the finest in London, is also recommended.

As an *envoi* to this chapter, it should never be forgotten that the rural station, the wayside signal-box, were built to be seen in a particular setting, and that the country can hardly claim to show any reverence for better builders than today's when the annual total which it expends from government funds on the *in situ* preservation of *all* its ancient buildings is little over half a million pounds out of a total 'arts' budget of more than ten million. It is not suggested that British Railways should add the financial responsibility for architectural preservation to their other responsibilities, though they could certainly show a less philistine and puritanical approach to the subject. (It is interesting that two writers on railway architecture quoted above, Michael Robbins and Christian Barman, were associated with railway public relations in the days when their past was still regarded with pride: it would be even more interesting to hear these writers' comments on the present annual vandalism). But this is a matter for the national conscience.

If railway architecture—if the architecture of the whole British industrial revolution—received one tenth of the total quoted above for purposes of preservation it would be fortunate; and £50,000 is, at current rates, the price only of the salaries of a couple of chairmen of nationalised industries, one new production of a Covent Garden opera (plus a few subsidies to 'experimental' theatres, or less than half a painting distinguishable from a fair copy only by mechanical tests. It might also be a good deal less than the tourist revenue which the nation could earn once it began fully to appreciate the richness of its heritage of industrial architecture.

PART THREE

# *LOCOMOTION*

## *VII ENGINES ON ICE*

In August 1968—considerably earlier than was expected even a decade before—there ran the last standard-gauge steam locomotives owned by British Railways. As will be seen in the next chapter, the qualifications suggested by this statement are important. But this rather inglorious occasion from which the BR Pacific No 70013, *Oliver Cromwell*, departed towards a republican immortality at Bressingham Hall, did mark the end of the era of main-line steam—an era which had lasted for over a century and a half and had brought to perfection the only machine ever to inspire a large section of mankind, generation after generation, with a mixture of respect and love. It also implied that thenceforth *every* steam locomotive must be regarded as an historic relic.

The speculation made earlier in this book, as to how long the mystique of steam—a mystique reflected not only in toys and children's books but in popular artefacts of every kind—will survive the passing of the reality, is especially relevant here. But the steam locomotive will always have its devotees, and these will be saved from complete frustration by the types of preservation which form the subject of these next chapters—static in museum collections, and dynamic for the locomotives still active in special circumstances.

These two forms are complementary and not quite mutually exclusive; for locomotive-running societies often have their own museums and most statically-preserved engines are not mere mummies but in full working order down to their fire-tubes. Nor is railworthiness necessarily proportional to age, though some of the historic survivors still operative are largely so on the principle of the former's axe which remained as good as new thanks to seven new blades and twelve new hafts. But inevitably the static collections contain most of the earliest relics and of the heavy and historic main-liners of greatest interest to serious engineers (and power to impress schoolboys), whilst the operating groups are largely concerned with local curiosities on the one hand and with sound, steamable engines on the other.

It is for this reason that the dead (or, at least, sleeping) are here described before the quick. But first the general recent background to the preservation of Britain's locomotives—and, with them, of a good deal of other *railwayana*—should be noted. For this subject has given rise to understandable puzzlement and misapprehension, particularly amongst overseas visitors.

With the 1923 amalgamation the four great railway groups inherited a miscellany of railway objects, including 26 locomotives, which had been with varying thoroughness (and sometimes almost absent-mindedly) preserved by their predecessors. For the most part they left these in the obscurity of their engine-sheds and paint shops—where they were added to from time to time—or preserved at scattered sites. But in 1928 one company, the LNER, converted part of the historic old station of York into the world's first railway museum. Nominally, this was a regional collection; but in fact it provided a home for such similar relics from other parts of the British Isles as did not find their way to the national Science Museum in South Kensington, London, the sub-national museums of Scotland (Edinburgh) and Wales (Cardiff), and the municipal collections of regional centres which have since been joined by a new generation of county council establishments. Hence York became, in the public mind, '*the* railway museum'.

An ill-conceived act of nationalisation in 1948 brought not only the railways but a good many other transport undertakings under one body, the British Transport Commission. At the head of this in an age of some confidence, Sir Brian Robertson noted that numerous countries now had national railway or transport museums and resolved that Britain should own the best such. The York collection would remain, and indeed was to be supplemented by other regional museums. (In the event only one small one was opened, at Swindon: this, which was housed in a former chapel, received municipal support and has now been presented to the local authority). But a new office of the BTC—the department of historical relics—would be set up, and would aim not only at a general custodianship over all worthy material (*in situ* as well as portable) but at a London museum better than the housing then afforded by Nine Elms.

This target was achieved in 1961 when the so-called Museum of British Transport was opened in a disused but modern bus garage off the High Street of Clapham, SW4: its entrance is now marked by a model of the *Rocket*, and is a few minutes from Clapham Common underground station. In many ways the premises formed a better compromise that could have been expected, though it is hard not to compare their essentially makeshift nature with the establishment of the great London museums of the Victorian age. The ex-garage, after all, *did* provide cover and (rather limited) space for 100-ton locomotives; and though Clapham was not a fashionable address it was almost as near to the heart of London as was Kensington.

This was, however, a British *Transport* enterprise; and the BTC also had under its wing the waterways and London's municipal transport system—though it had little else to do with road travel, with the sea (except for railway steamers), or with the air. Clapham's interests were not logically chosen but politically imposed and hardly had its miscellany been appraised than a change of government brought about the dismemberment of the unwieldy BTC and the reclassification of its million-odd relics under the British Railways Board.

Shortly afterwards the canal material departed to a pleasant and appropriate waterside home at Stoke Bruerne, Northants. But Clapham was still left holding London Transport's baby, which of course belonged—together with the best of the stage coaches and vintage Rolls which are at present scattered through dozens of private and public collections—in a separate road transport museum. It obviously had to hold on, too, to the ex-railway-ship's bells which should have been in the National Maritime collection, and could only be thankful that aviation has barely entered into its bailiwick.

So an exercise in national transport planning ended in one more British muddle. A greater tragedy, though, was that even in its proper field this establishment which had now inherited the 'railway museum' title had lost ground. The railways were in financial difficulties, and the accountants and salesmen who succeeded Robertson not only negatively begrudged money spent on commemorating the past but positively encouraged the severance of historic links in their search for new 'images'. And though the historical relics department could not be wound up (the Clapham museum itself was proving increasingly popular, though it never became financially self-supporting), it *could* be told that its budget would be insufficient for its needs and that the architectural recommendations with which it was originally charged must take second place to the economic utilisation of assets—ie were not worth making. At the same period, the civic provincial museums became equally hard-pressed for staff and display-space.

The latest phase in this story is that a dying government has proposed to 'regroup' as much as possible of the railway contents of the Clapham collection at York. Twenty years before the socialist catch-phrase had been centralisation: now it was regional planning. Should this move take place, the loss to the nation would be considerable even apart from the fact that locomotives and carriages long and carefully preserved might have to be scrapped and would certainly be sold-off: the place for a reference collection is in a nation's capital and York, for all its charms, is remote from tourist routes, short on facilities, and visited largely by bishops. This scheme—which would virtually denude London of railway material and whose only positive feature is the recognition that railway preservation should be a charge on the national purse rather than BR funds—must be re-thought.

But for the time, at least, we have Clapham, which includes in its railway exhibits (and visitors can either take in the anomalous buses and ships' models or leave them alone) the world's richest and most imaginatively-displayed collection of locomotives—most of them inherited from days long before amalgamation, but with a number which entered the collection directly from their retirement. We have the older York and the younger Swindon displays, together with a few locomotives still on their pedestals in local stations and (unfortunately) a larger group, classified as 'stored' by the BRB, which can only be inspected by prior arrangement. We also have a selection of engines at South Kensington (which houses some important early ones) and in various regional, civic and other museums—two or three of which, indeed, have established transport sections of their own even when their engines are not yet on show. And in addition a number of major locomotives are in the hands of private societies and individuals;

for the most part these are referred to in the next chapter, since they are generally held with a view to restoration to service even if not currently steaming.

As a further complication, several of the scattered exhibits are in fact BRB property out on permanent loan as a residue of the original and ambitious concept of a national centre of railway (or even transport) lore. This point, though apparently academic, is made because the phrase 'BRB collection' has been used earlier in this book. This is normally synonymous with display at Clapham unless otherwise stated; but certain smaller relics are still rehoused from time to time, whilst reciprocally some of the Board's exhibits are loaned by other authorities. Even many locomotives have—quite apart from the threat of York—probably not yet finished their travels: in recent years, for instance, the BRB has as an economy measure lent several major engines to regional museums and even individuals.

Perhaps this is fitting for objects which were born to move. In a more practical mood, it should be noted that in general the locomotives mentioned in both this and the next chapter are restored to the state and livery of their heydays and complete with contemporary tenders. Prior to about 1835, of course, the 'tender' was just a barrel and heap of coke on a flat-car.

The excursion train, having visited country which demanded to be explored somewhere in this book, now returns to its home station as the listing of Britain's 120-odd statically-preserved locomotives begins. This chapter cannot, of course, enter into technical specifications of cylinder bores and firegrate areas or relate the engines' full (and, in many cases, colourful) history: for all such information, including details of numberings after those of the original operating company, the locomotive-lover is referred to H. C. Casserley's standard work and the publications of 'Forum' and of Hugh Evelyn, Ltd. It is intended rather as a guide to present locations; but perhaps it should begin with a sense of gratitude that so much has been saved through so many vicissitudes. Until the last few years locomotives were preserved almost by hazard; but though every enthusiast will have his own regrets for what has been lost (no standard-gauge Beyer-Garratt, nothing by the older Trevithick, nothing from the London, Chatham and Dover, no *Decapod*, no *Cardean*), one's first reaction *must* be one of thanks that so wide a range of important engines have survived, particularly from the first hundred years of steam, to represent the thousands of classes and modifications which once ran on Britain's rails.

The oldest survivors of all are the twins which William Hedley and Timothy Hackworth built at Wylam colliery in 1813. The wheel arrangements of both were modified early in their active lives, but not the trelliswork of overhead connecting and valve rods which, inherited from beam-engine practice, took the place of the simple chain or gear drives of even earlier experiments. One of these predecessors—*Puffing Billy*, preserved in the Science Museum—forms part of British mythology: her less renowned but slightly older sister, *Wylam Dilly* (which at one stage of her career was used as a tug-boat engine) is housed in the Royal Scottish Museum, Edinburgh 1. (Plate 26). It is largely thanks to the efforts of their Newcastle builders that both have been preserved for over 150 years; and perhaps it is churlish to feel that one would swap either of them with oblivion for the sake of, say, a Blenkinsop and Murray original, for only the wheels of one of these latter survive at York.

From the next decade three industrial locomotives have endured—one from the Hetton colliery line, the high-chimneyed *Agenoria* from the vanished Shutt End railway near Stourbridge, Worcs, and a last from Killingworth colliery. The first—by George Stephenson, who built the line itself in the same year of 1822—is preserved by the BRB at York (Plate 26); the second, by Foster and Rastrick in 1829, is also at York but loaned by the Science Museum: and the third, by the Stephensons again (1832) is at the Museum of Science and Engineering, Exhibition Park, Newcastle (Plate 27). All are four-wheeled, as are five more famous public-railway locomotives which have also been miraculously preserved from this still formative age.

The senior of this group is Hackworth's *Locomotion*, built for the Stockton and Darlington in 1825 and now preserved, together with a contemporary tender, at Darlington (Bank Top) station (Plate 27). Of the engines which showed their paces before a crowd of 10,000 at Rainhill in 1829, the same builder's *Sans Pareil* and the more renowned *Rocket* of the Stephensons can be seen side by side (and manifestly belonging to the same stage of evolution of *eohippus ferri*) at the Science Museum. *Sans Pareil*, though, was somewhat rebuilt—as the first act of locomotive preservation—on her retirement; and *Rocket* was much modified in her lifetime, as comparison with a replica of her original state shows.

Both these locomotives entered public service in the next year. Another Rainhill entrant, the half-Swedish *Novelty*, blew herself up; but enough was salvaged for a rebuild to work on the St Helen's railway, and this *revenant* too is now at South Kensington. From the contemporary line in the south, the Canterbury and Whitstable railway, George Stephenson's *Invicta* of 1830 (whose works number followed that of the *Rocket*, and who was first driven by Edward Fletcher) is preserved in the open at Riding Gate, Canterbury (Plate 27).

The survivors from the first years of steam hence form an unexpectedly large and rich group. It is perhaps fortunate that the energies of the 1830s were directed more to the building of lines than to the improvement of locomotives, for relics of this decade are scant. There is, in fact, only one pure-bred (if somewhat mysterious) survivor, the *Lion* of 1838 who remained steamable well over a century later when she headed the *Titfield Thunderbolt*. Built by Kitsons for the L&M, this represents the oldest surviving engine with more than 4 wheels, being a 0–4–2. She is owned by a Liverpool engineering society, but with her high chimney and great square firebox is temporarily housed in store.

The paucity of exhibits from this age of timber-clad boilers can in part be traced to the lack of historic sense of so thrustful a period; but later ages too have taken their toll. Until 1905, for instance, two of the earliest locomotives built for the broad gauge lurked in the Swindon sheds: then, the GWR being notably iconoclastic, they were broken up by Churchward

PLATE 25

Above is a brave showing of steam as A3 *Flying Scotsman* climbs above Hawick with an enthusiasts' special. Her designer, Sir Nigel Gresley, is also remembered by the eponymous A4, (below), at present held in store with roughened smoothing and other later accretions.

PLATE 26

Two breeds of *eohippus ferri*—Hedley's *Wylam Dilly* of 1813 (above) and George Stephenson's Hetton Colliery locomotive of 1822 (right).

PLATE 27

Some other predecessors—(left top) Hackworth's *Locomotion* at Darlington station–note scenery; (left bottom) Stephenson's Killingworth colliery engine supporting his statue at Newcastle; and *Invicta* by the same builder somewhat disrespectfully displayed at Canterbury (below).

PLATE 28

Industrial locomotives preserved at Birmingham include the narrow-gauge *Lorna Doone* (above) and *Secundus* of 1874 (below).

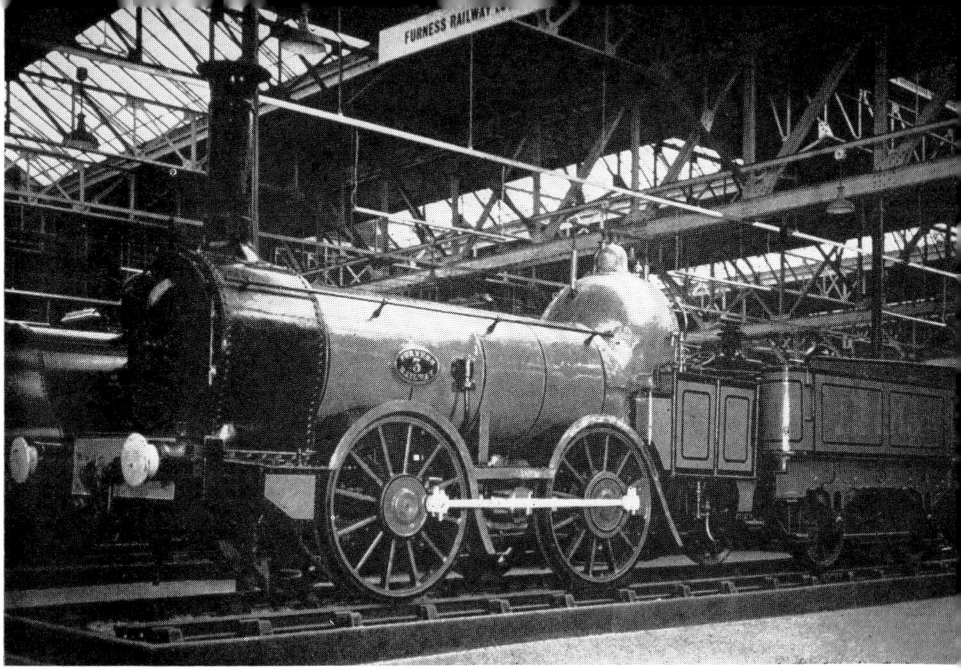

PLATE 29

These locomotives from the BRB collection span thirty years of building and a century of service. They comprise Bury's *Copper Nob* from the Furness railway (above: 1846-1898, Clapham), Fletcher's No 910 from the NER (below: 1875-1925, York), and the Beyer, Peacock A Class condensing engine from the Metropolitan Railway (bottom: 1866-1948, Clapham).

PLATE 30

Two magnificent 'singles' preserved by the BRB—the LNWR's much-rebuilt *Cornwall* (above, at Clapham) and the GNR's No 1 by Patrick Stirling (below, at York).

PLATE 31 Also preserved at York is (above) Stroudley's LBSCR *Gladstone* of 1882. One of the same designer's 'Terriers', *Newington*, below, finds a new use as a pub sign on Hayling Island, Hants.

PLATE 32

A narrow-gauge selection. The historic 4 ft gauge *Fire Queen* of 1848 (above left) awaits her next move in North Wales while (above right) *Pixie* (with the Rev. E. R. Boston up) and *Gwynydd* (below), both of contractors' gauge, steam in their own backyards at Cadeby Rectory and Bressingham Hall respectively.

to make space. It was left to a later age to reassemble what little was left of George Stephenson's 2–2–2 *North Star* of 1837 (one leather buffer was found being used as a door-stop) into the part-replica now preserved at Swindon.

This is perhaps not quite so 'meaningless' as LTC Rolt claims, but it is certainly small compensation for the loss of the original, which was itself one of the two engines which kept the Bristol line rolling in its earliest years. The only other survivor of the broad gauge is the quite untypical *Tiny* of 1868, a vertical-boilered 0–4–0 inspection-train tank engine from the south Devon railway preserved at Newton Abbot station and itself in a largely reconstructed state.

One other engine possibly belongs to the 1830s, since a Hackworth locomotive for the Stockton and Darlington—*Derwent* or No 25, also preserved at Darlington station—is dated by Nock as early as 1838 though by the BRB at 1845 (part of a similar locomotive still existing at Hetton colliery certainly goes back to 1835). In either case she is of considerable interest, though less because her six wheels are fabricated in the peculiar form imposed by Shildon's lack of a lathe with a 4 ft. capacity than for the general neatness of appearance. *Derwent* appears to have been *designed* rather than (like her predecessors) merely assembled, and so provides a suitable introduction to the next generation of locomotives which entered service from the mid-1840s onwards.

Visible hallmarks of this age were horizontal cylinders at frame level, the simplification of an earlier profusion of brass-encased domes, valves and whistles, prominent lamps and leather buffers, the improvement of the driving platform as it very slowly developed into a true cab, and the evolution of company liveries—for all locomotives hitherto had been of natural finishes or painted black or in the lines's favourite colour combination of the moment. But, more important, was the search for greater adhesive power and, in passenger service, for speed. For the inadequacies of the earlier type of 0–4–0 when pressed into trunk-route service had been shown by the career of Edward Bury, who powered—and under-powered—three early main lines.

One of Bury's last designs, however, not only had the distinctive appearance lent by a cylindrical, domed and unpainted firebox and long clean boiler but gave good service on (*inter alia*) the Furness Railway. This type is represented in the BRB collection by No 3, who was nicknamed rather than christened *Copper Nob*. Built in 1846 at Liverpool, she was long on display at Barrow-in-Furness but is now at Clapham (Plate 29).

By coincidence the two other survivors from this decade also begin with the third letter of the alphabet, as if to stress that they belong to a third generation of locomotives with sophisticated arrangements including proper tenders. Of these, the extremely elegant 2–2–2 *Columbine* was built at Crewe (the first engine ever to leave that centre) to the designs of Alexander Allen in 1845: numbered 49, she entered service on the Grand Junction railway from Birmingham to Warrington, ran for nearly sixty years, and is now preserved at York. Two years later, when this line had entered the LNWR complex, William Trevithick built *Cornwall* as that company's locomotive No 173: another 2–2–2, she was to remain in leisurely service until 1935—a career of some 86 years. Although Hamilton Ellis has found her original Cramptonish design 'freakish', the result of John Ramsbottom's rebuild of 1858 is most impressive, with the splashers over the 8 ft. 6 in. driving wheels towering almost to the top of the boiler (Plate 30).

Such 'singles' were to form the aristocrats of passenger locomotion for several decades to come. But from the recession years of the 1850s not one important survivor remains, even Mr. Crampton's patents failing on their home ground though at least one is preserved overseas. This period would in fact be unrepresented were it not for a light railway.

It has already been suggested that this last phrase covers several ideas—the narrow-gauge line, the mineral tramway and the inter-urban electric tram being among them. Even after the Acts of the 1870s, however, the steam-worked, unfenced roadside railway once common on the continent remained rare in Britain. (The motive power of this group is represented at Clapham by one very curious survivor from a very curious line, a geared Aveling and Porter from the originally-private, six-mile enterprise hopefully called Oxford and Aylesbury tramroad of 1872). But the station-to-town spur at Wantage, Berks.—a much-loved little line—took over an older locomotive which became its No 5, *Shannon*. A diminutive 0–4–0WT of 1853, she was formerly housed at Wantage Road but is now (with the closure of the main-line station) being stored pending display on a site in the heart of King Alfred's town.

From 1865 onwards the number of engines preserved rises steadily with the decades as assured, fourth-generation locomotives take over. Many, however, are of the smaller types in which the BRB collection is, over this period, particularly rich. It includes, for instance, an LNWR 0–4–0 shunter by Ramsbottom, No 1439 of 1865 (housed in the Staffordshire County Council's industrial collection at Shugborough Hall, Staffs, whose larger railway exhibits are not yet on display); a well-known but much-rebuilt 4–4–0 of the next year of the influential A class, No 23 by Beyer Peacock, whose condenser and vent pipes witness her use on the underground Metropolitan Railway and who saw 82 years of service (Plate 29); and the Midland's hard-worked No 158A—a Matthew Kirtley class 156 express 2–4–0. Also of 1866, this has been loaned to the Leicester museum and is now exhibited in the former tram-shed in Stoneygate.

*Aerolite*, a North Eastern 2–2–4T built by Kitsons and now preserved at York, is usually given the birth-year of 1869 since she then received at the hands of Edward Fletcher the most radical of her three reconstructions: she was to suffer several later rebuildings and a change of wheel formula, however, and had in fact made her debut at the Great Exhibition of 1851. An unusual survivor at Shugborough is a section of an 0–6–0 built for the Oxford, Worcester and Wolverhampton railway in 1855 which was in 1904 cut up for instructional purposes; and two 0–4–0STs from the Furness railway, built by Sharp, Stewart in 1863 and 1865 as Nos 18 and 25, are privately preserved at local schools after having steamed for nearly a century.

If one name above others is associated with the steam locomotive's achievement of elegance it is that of Patrick Stirling of the Great Northern, and one should hence be grateful to time (and to Nigel Gresley) that No 1, the first of his immortal 4–2–2s with the 8 ft. driving wheel (class A2—the 'most-written, oftest-sung engines in British locomotive history', as Hamilton Ellis calls them) is still preserved at York—and is probably in steamable condition after the lapse of a century since her birth in 1870 (Plate 30). Slightly less glamorous survivors of this decade include two North-Eastern engines, No 1275 (an 0–6–0 of 1874) and No 910 (Plate 29), an ornate 2–4–0 of Edward Fletcher's 901 class built the next year with a typical smokebox door: both are now at York. From the South-Western came No 298, the prototype of W. G. Beattie's 2–4–0WT class of that number: built by Beyer Peacock in 1874, she was withdrawn from service 88 years later and is currently in store.

Two still humbler exhibits from the same year are *Bauxite No* 2, a Black, Hawthorn saddle-tank displayed in the Science Museum and (at the Museum of Science and Industry, Newhall Street, Birmingham) *Secundus*, an 0–6–0WT built for a Dorsetshire industrial tramway (Plate 31). But meanwhile, one of the most renowned types of smaller British locomotive had entered service, Stroudley's 0–6–0 tanks of the A1 (reboilered as A1X) class. Affectionately known for their liveliness as 'Terriers', these saw long and wide service on London, Brighton and South Coast and other branches. Thanks to their longevity, no fewer than ten of the original group of fifty have been preserved and generally restored to the designer's equally famous 'improved engine green' livery.

The BRB's representative of the class—the un-rebuilt No 82, *Boxhill*, of 1880—was used as a yard pilot until recently, but is now immobile at Clapham. Other 'Terriers' are preserved at a public house on Hayling Island, Hants (No 46 *Newington*, 1876—Plate 31) and by Butlin's holiday camps, an organisation which has shown a lively interest in serious locomotive preservation. It exhibits, for instance, No 40 (*Brighton*, 1878) at its Pwllheli camp, No 62 (*Martello*, 1875) at Ayr and No 78 (*Knowle*, 1880) at Minehead. Another Stroudley LBSC locomotive (preserved by the BRB at York—Plate 31) is No 214 of the B1 class of 0–4–2 passenger express engines: named *Gladstone*, she was built in 1882.

Also at York is No 1463 of the North Eastern's 2–4–0 class of the same number—probably the only type of British passenger express engine to have no official designer since built by committee-work in 1885 after Stirling's successor had resigned in anger, but often known as a "Tennant". The Mersey railway's powerful 0–6–4T No 5 *Cecil Raikes* of 1885, is currently held in store for the City of Liverpool museum in William Brown Street; and the same museum has reserved an 0–6–0ST built in 1906 for the Mersey Docks and Harbour Board, whose locomotive No 1 it was.

No 123 of the Caledonian railway, a unique 4–2–2 with 7 ft. driving wheels built to the design of Dugald Drummond by Neilsons in 1886, is not only the oldest preserved Scottish locomotive but was the last of all the 'singles' to see regular service since she worked as late as 1935. She represented the northern partner of the west coast route in the race to Scotland of 1888, and is now loaned by the BRB to the admirable Glasgow museum of transport in Albert Drive. A final officially-preserved survivor from this decade (unfortunately still in store) is John Aspinall's Lancashire and Yorkshire railway class 5 2–4–2 tank No 1008, built at Horwich in 1889 as the first to leave that works; but the unusual industrial museum at Penrhyn Castle in North Wales which is administered by the National Trust holds an 0–6–2 Webb 'coal tank' from the LNWR of 1888, No 1054.

The mention above of the Scottish races is a reminder of the sophistication which came to passenger locomotive design in the 1880s. But the "singles" were now enjoying only an Indian summer, and the next passenger express locomotive preserved by the BRB (and associated with the second series of races, those to Aberdeen in 1895) is a 2–4–0. A member of the fearsome Francis Webb's LNWR "Precedent" or "Jumbo" class, she is No 790, *Hardwicke*. Apparently built at Crewe in 1892, she has also been accorded a much earlier date.

One of her rivals on the east coast run was Wilson Worsdell's (and the North-Eastern's handsome M1 class 4–4–0, No 1621 of 1893, now preserved at York. The South Western is represented by a particularly wide range from the years of classic design, with an Adams O2 class 0–4–4T of 1891, No 209, privately kept on the Isle of Wight, a T3 4–4–0 of 1893, No 563, at Clapham, a B4 0–4–0T of the same year, No 102, at Butlin's, Skegness, and two Dugald Drummond locomotives held in store by the BRB—No 245, an 0–4–4T of the large M7 class of 1897, and a T9 4–4–0, No 120, which was built in 1899 and steamed until 1963.

From the Midland at this period came No 118, a class 115 4–2–2: built in 1897 as the last of the elegant Samuel Johnson "spinner" singles, she has been loaned by the BRB to the Leicester museum and is on show at Stoneygate. The Great Eastern has contributed No 490 of James Holden's large T29 class of 2–4–0s built in 1894 to be preserved at Clapham, and the Great Northern No 990, *Henry Oakley*, a "Klondyke" 4–4–2 of 1898 belonging to the C2 class of Ivatt Atlantics which rather illogically preceded the more powerful and numerous C1s. She is exhibited at York.

The Highland railway's oldest preserved locomotive—now displayed by the Glasgow transport museum—is No 103 of 1894, a 4–6–0 of the class which is possibly miscalled "Jones Goods" but which was certainly the first in Britain to use this wheel arrangement. Also in this museum (and presented to it by a local fund) is a neat Caledonian railway 0–6–0 of 1899, No 828 of the 812 class; designed by J. F. McIntosh, she represents the freight equivalents of the long-vanished "Dunalastairs".

For reasons already mentioned, Great Western survivors from the last century are pitifully few. The only one which can be introduced without qualification, indeed, is a humble 0–6–0 of the 2301 or "Dean Goods" class—No 2516, built in 1897 when the type was already becoming obsolete, and now exhibited at Swindon. From the company's Taff Vale associate, however, a 01 class 0–6–2T—No 28 of the same year—survived an eventful career to end up by being preserved on behalf of the BRB by the

South Wales Switchgear Co, Caerphilly, Glam., where she awaits restoration. And from the Cardiff railway No 5, an 0–4–0ST built by Kitsons in 1898 and later bearing the GWR number 1338, has been privately preserved at Bleadon and Uphill station, Somerset.

With the opening of the present century, too, the Great Western comes into its own in terms of locomotive preservation just as it did historically in terms of speed. The two aspects are fused in the case of No 3440, the immortal 3700 or "City" class 4–4–0 *City of Truro* which, built in 1903, was almost certainly the first locomotive to exceed 100 mph in the Plymouth boat-train races. She is of course preserved at Swindon, as is her descendant the 4–6–0 *Lode Star* of 1907—No 4003 of the 4000 or "Star" class. A heavy freight 2–8–0—No 2818 of the long-lived 28 class, built in 1905—has been presented to the City Museum, Queens Road, Bristol 8, where she is now in store together with three industrial 0–6–0STs from local builders; and the Leicester collection includes No 921, an 0–4–0T built in 1906 for industrial service and later Great-Westernised.

With a new century whose early years formed the golden age of locomotive design one is increasingly dealing with engines still operative in the final days of steam. Thus, the South-Eastern and Chatham railway's D class No 737, Wainwright's elegant and ornate 4–4–0 passenger express locomotive of 1901 now preserved at Clapham, was not retired until 1956; the London, Tilbury and Southend's Whitelegg 79 class 4–4–2T No 80 of 1909, *Thundersley*, made a final commemorative run in the same year (and will probably make further brief forays, since she has been loaned to the private museum of Bressingham Hall, Diss, Norfolk and there provided with a short track); a Holden Great Eastern 0–6–0T No 87 (1904: Clapham) operated until 1960; and the same company's tender 0–6–0 class No 1217 of 1905 (in BRB store) worked until 1962. Slightly shorter-lived were the Great Northern's first C1 Ivatt Atlantic—No 251, built in 1902 and at that time the largest engine in the country, and the Midland's No 1000, a modified version of the first of Johnson's compound 4–4–0s which appeared in the same year. The former is preserved at York, and the latter at Clapham.

Only two other publicly-preserved engines seem to date from before the outbreak of the first world war and the centenary of the building of the first preserved locomotives. These are the Great Central railway's Robinson class 8K 2–8–0 No 102 (now loaned by the BRB to the Leicester collection, but not yet on display), and a class K 4–4–0 from the North British railway—No 256, *Glen Douglas*, preserved by the Glasgow transport museum. The exact birth-year of both is curiously uncertain, and the "Glen" may in fact be of post-war construction.

Another Scottish locomotive, the only one surviving from the Glasgow and South Western railway, is also the only preserved main-liner of wartime building. She is the much-travelled No 9, an 0–6–0T of Peter Drummond's 322 class, built in 1917 and—naturally enough—also preserved at Glasgow. In the Industrial Museum of South Wales, Swansea, there is a fireless Barclay 0–4–0 built for oil refinery use in 1916.

By 1919 the noonday light was fading from Britain's railways; but five locomotives remain to witness the last few years when a dozen or so companies retained their independent traditions of design. In 1919, for instance, the North Eastern built the first of its huge 0–8–0 Q7 class—No 901, now stored by the BRB. 1920 saw the birth of the Great Central's fine "11F" class of 4–4–0s designed by J. G. Robinson and named (as was the GCR's modest habit) after directors of the line: of these *Butler Henderson*—No 506, now at Clapham—was destined for preservation. The same year produced another 4–4–0 and another sole survivor which now completes the Glasgow museum's representation of the north-of-the-border companies, the Great North of Scotland's class F No 49 *Gordon Highlander*. Designed by T. E. Heywood, her looks are worthy of the splendour of her own, and her company's, names.

In 1921 the LNWR produced its G2 class 0–8–0 No 485: now loaned to store in Leicester, she represents a type which was for three decades to demonstrate the superiority of Crewe over Derby design for heavy freight engines. And in the last year of the old regime a company not hitherto represented—for its stud was liquidated soon after amalgamation—makes an appearance. This was the North Staffordshire railway which built (not in time to steam *under* their own colour of madder-lake, though she did so *in* them) the 0–6–2 tank of J. H. Adams' L class, No 2, now preserved for the BRB in the Shugborough Hall collection. This also houses an 0–4–0ST built for a Burton brewery in 1921.

The first of the post-amalgamation engines to be officially preserved (for she was completed in August, 1923) is in several ways historic. She came, for instance, from the Great Western, the company which had not merely had a continuous tradition of locomotive design for some forty years but which was to pass comparatively unchanged and untroubled by internal jealousies through the years of the "big four" groups. She was herself an heir of the "Star" class of nearly two decades before: she was to give rise to distinguished descendants: and her own type was to continue to be reproduced for nearly thirty years more, as well as to influence the design of still later passenger express locomotives. Finally, she was destined to be the only representative of the large, 'modern' steam locomotive in the Science Museum, where she will doubtless be marvelled at by future millions of schoolboys who will never see another such machine—particularly if the BRB collection leaves London. She is, of course, the first of Collett's 4–6–0s of the 4073, "Castle" class, *Caerphilly Castle*, last seen in steam in 1960.

The earliest preserved locomotive (now stored at Leicester) of that then-new Goliath the London, Midland and Scottish railway, is an example of a ubiquitous 4F group of heavy 0–6–0s, No 4027: though built in 1924 she follows a design of Fowler's dating from 1911 and with roots nearly forty years earlier still. Two Southern railway 4–6–0s dating from 1925 and 1926 (and now in BRB store) were, however, substantially new types even though the first—No E777 of the N17 or "King Arthur" class, *Sir Lamiel*—was developed by Maunsell from an LSWR design. The other is *Lord Nelson*, the 'flagship' of that class and No E850.

The Royal Scottish museum, Edinburgh, hopes shortly to have on display an interesting early Gresley 4–4–0 engine, class D49 No 246 *Morayshire*, of 1928. A more famous locomotive of the same year is the first built (and almost the last to survive) of the next enlargement of GWR design, the 6000 or "King" class 4–6–0s which in their time were Britain's most powerful passenger engines. *King George V*, of course, achieved particular fame through the transatlantic loan which gave her her memorial bell, and has not yet finished her travels. For after a period on display at Swindon she has been loaned to Bulmer's cider company, who intend to exhibit (and possibly steam) her at Hereford, together with three Pullman carriages.

An equally renowned engine was the LMS 6P No 6100 *Royal Scot*. Built in 1927 to Henry Fowler's design (which was itself hurriedly based on the "Lord Nelsons"), she travelled widely in the USA, was later completely rebuilt by William Stanier, and is preserved at Butlins camp at Skegness. A gap of seven years separates her from two other LMS locomotives, No 2500—a Stanier 4P 2–6–4T designed for the Southend line and No 5000, the first-built and official representative of the enormously popular class '5', "Black Stanier" 4–6–0s. Both are in BRB store, the latter being destined for the forthcoming Leicester museum.

1934 also saw the debut of the last of the typically-British 4–4–0 types, the Southern's V or "Schools" class; of these, No 925 *Cheltenham*, is stored by the BRB, whilst No 926 *Stowe*,—is preserved by Lord Montagu in his museum at Beaulieu, Hants, which is more commonly associated with vintage cars: she is there accompanied by three more-or-less contemporaneous Pullman coaches from the *Bournemouth Belle*. A GWR 0–4–2T, built in 1935 as No 1442, is displayed opposite the goods station in Blundell's Road, Tiverton, Devon, having been presented to a town which houses some smaller railway exhibits in its museum.

The later 1930s form a St Martin's summer of steam, dominated by the two northern systems who had now to fight not only each other but road and air transport for the Scottish traffic. Classic Stanier LMS Pacifics of this period which have been preserved include three held by Butlin's—*Princess Margaret Rose* (7P No 6203, 1935, at Pwllheli), the Atlantic-crossing *Duchess of Hamilton* (No 6229 of the heavier "Coronation" version, 1938, at Minehead), and *Duchess of Sutherland* (No 6233 of the same year, a twin sister except that she was never sullied with the streamlining later removed from milady Hamilton) at Ayr. And the BRB has presented to the museum of her name-town, where she is not yet on display, *City of Birmingham*, No 6235 of the same group but built in 1937 as a streamlined engine. Unlike the rest of the class, she is preserved in BR and not LMS livery.

The LNER's counterparts are less numerous in public collections but are certainly no less impressive. For these include not only a class V2 2–6–2 No 4771 of 1936—*Green Arrow*, now stored on BRB loan at Laicester—but another of the immortals, A4 No 4468, *Mallard*. Of all the Gresley 4–6–2s, it was of course she who won the ultimate laurel of steam after a century of progress by attaining the now-unbreakable world record of over 126 mph shortly after completion in 1938. She is enshrined at Clapham.

Some would consider the collapse of standards brought about by war conditions to be epitomised by the Austerity Q1 0–6–0s which Bulleid then built for the Southern railway. Yet grotesque as the prototype—No 1 of 1942—appears by comparison with her predecessors, she now has the period charm of a *Picture Post* photograph of a socialite in a siren-suit. This gallant if unlovely lady is in BRB store. An industrial locomotive built by Pecketts in the previous year, 0–4–0ST No 2004, is stored by the Birmingham museum.

A final SR engine—also in store for the moment—represents Bulleid's 4–6–2 (or, as he put it, 21C) "Battle of Britain" and "West Country" classes. She is the un-rebuilt, air-smoothed No 15 *Sir Winston Churchill* of 1945, one of whose last tasks was to haul the ex-premier's funeral train. Together with the founder member (No 9400, built in 1947) of the GWR's humble but much-loved 0–6–0 pannier-tank shunters formally preserved at Swindon, she completes the list of locomotives built by the independent companies and now in public hands, though some earlier designs were of course multiplied in the British Railways era. For instance, a representative of Henry Ivatt's good-looking class 2 2–6–0s, now privately preserved but destined for the museum of Dundee, was built in 1950 as BR No 46464.

But this new complex also produced a final range of its own. Representatives of two of its largest types have been officially preserved (though not yet displayed), of which No 70000 *Britannia*—a 4–6–2 which named the mixed-traffic class 7—was the first of all to be built. It would be interesting to see if she still carries plates saying "Built Crewe 1950, rebuilt Swindon 1951." No 92220, *Evening Star* is a 9F class freight 2–10–0: constructed at Swindon in 1960, she was dedicated from the start for preservation as the last steam locomotive to be built for the main lines of Britain. Only five years later, after a minor accident, she was withdrawn from service. She hence illustrates not only the final sophistication of locomotive design (and the difficulties of publicly displaying all the later survivors of the age of steam) but the short-sighted decisions which have dogged the British Railways era.

This chapter has hitherto been concerned entirely with standard-gauge locomotives. However, the Birmingham collection also includes the 2 ft. gauge *Leonard* No 2087, a 0–4–0ST built by Bagnalls in 1919 for a local drainage board, and *Lorna Doone* (Kerr Stuart, 1922, from a chalk quarry of Barnstaple (Plate 28), whilst at present immured at Llanberis, Caernarvon—but destined for the museum at Penrhyn Castle—there is a most handsome and unusual 4 ft. gauge 0–4–0, *Fire Queen*, dating back to 1848. (Plate 32) Furthermore, the last few years have seen the expansion of a museum which, though an offshoot of the Talyllyn railway mentioned in the next chapter, may now be counted a national collection representing that very diffuse entity, the British narrow-gauge tradition.

In fact, the terms of reference of this collection at Wharf Station, Towyn, Merioneth, are even wider, since it houses not only "No 13"—a remarkable 1 ft. 10 in. 0–4–0 of 1895 from the equally remarkable spiral railway at the Guinness brewery in Dublin off which a similar locomotive, complete with converter for broad-gauge working, is privately preserved at Brockham,

Surrey—but also *Cambrai.* This is an 0–6–0T of 1888 who spent her most active years on the metre-gauge Chemins de Fer du Cambresis before ending them on an English steelworks railway. Alone of the locomotives preserved in Britain she represents a European tradition, though several working engines are by American builders.

The narrow gauge museum (which is open through the summer season or by appointment) also houses some interesting rolling-stock, such as a host wagon for carrying 1 ft. 10¾ in. cars over a 4 ft. gauge 'main-line', and a wide range of miscellaneous material. Its most typical exhibits, however, are three locomotives from local slate mines—*George Henry* (Plate 38), a 1 ft. 11 in. 0–4–0T with a vertical boiler built in 1877 for the Penrhyn quarry line (two similar ones are privately preserved); *Jubilee 1897*, an 0–4–0ST by Manning Wardle (the year hardly needs restating) for another Caernarvonshire quarry, this time theoretically of 1 ft. 11½ in. gauge; and *Rough Pup* of 1891, also an 0–4–0ST, by Hunslet for the Dinorwic quarries (1 ft. 10½ in.).

Scotland is represented by an 0–4–0WT, No 2, built by Kerr Stuart to a design by Dugald Drummond in 1902 for service at a Dundee gasworks and again using that gauge of around 1 ft. 11 in. which corresponds to the continental 'contractors' or Decauville 600 mm. track. Curious as all these are, though, they are no less odd than the English contribution. For this comprises the smallest locomotives ever built for serious work.

In the final third of the last century, at least three locomotive works had systems laid on a 1 ft. 6 in. gauge to facilitate inter-factory movements. These were equipped with their own home-built steam engines which worked as late as 1963—tiny affairs with driving wheels only a few inches in diameter and footplates just big enough for a man to stand on, yet built with a meticulous workmanship which suggests that they may have been largely apprentice exercises. They were all christened, with diminutive names, and greatly loved; and fortunately three have survived.

These include *Pet*, an 0–4–0 from Crewe of 1865 whose tank might be described better as a tower than a saddle, and *Dot* of 1887, an 0–4–0WT by Beyer Peacock with a dome almost as big as her boiler and a jolly profusion of brassware. Both have been permanently loaned to the narrow-gauge museum by their builders. There they will complement another Beyer Peacock engine of 1887—the saddle-tanked *Wren*, who was built for the Lancashire and Yorkshire railway's works and is currently preserved at Clapham.

These form, perhaps, a strange finale to a survey which has included Stirling singles and 'Terriers', 'Kings' and A4s and other classics. But, even more vividly than the mighty, they bring home the reliance of a long century of British technology on the motive power of steam.

# VIII STILL IN STEAM

STEAM locomotives on pedestals—bright-painted, metal-polished, clean, bright and slightly oiled—are elegant things, and appear as they rarely did since they first left their makers' shops between 20 and 160 years ago. But even when technically steamable they are dead locomotives, *stuffed* locomotives. And to leave their company for that of their still-active cousins is to leave the natural history museum for Regent's Park, Whipsnade or even Longleat.

Unfortunately, the final step—to study the beasts in their natural habitat and under truly free-ranging conditions, which in this analogy means running in fast main-line service—is becoming a harder achievement than a safari to an African game reserve, for steam can now rarely be seen in action outside a variety of special branches of various types. Before passing on to this multiplicity of private lines, though, it should be remembered that BR itself is still—just—in the steam-hauled passenger railway business.

Of all the eccentric little lines which were acquired by big companies, only one has stood the test of time. But this continues to stand it, and would indeed be in an even more viable condition were the nationalised railways to show the commercial acumen of the private groups. For the Vale of Rheidol line operates only a short season and a very restricted service.

Running inland for eleven miles from Aberystwyth (Cardiganshire) to Devil's Bridge, this was opened as late as 1902 on the popular Welsh gauge of 1 ft. 11½ in. It was even then suspected that the lead ore at its terminus would prove an insufficient basis for profit, and the tourist trade was hence aimed at from the start. Of the three 2–6–2T locomotives which work the line, Nos 7 and 8 (*Owain Glyndwr* and *Llywelyn*) were built in 1923; but No 9, *Prince of Wales*, though remodelled at the same period, dates back to the opening year. These are among the handsomer of narrow-gauge locomotives; but together with the more modern coaches they have recently been repainted in the monotonous and inappropriate BR blue, as ludicrously unimaginative an example of standardised image-making as could be conceived.

Another Welsh concern, though owned throughout its history by a private but profit-earning company, has strong main-line links; for the Snowdon Mountain railway up from Llanberis (Caernarvon) was built in answer to Richard Moon's boast that he would carry the LNWR to the highest point in Britain south of the border. This prosperous and quite substantial little line, which climbs for just short of five miles to just under 3,500 ft. above sea level, has several claims to uniqueness: it is, for instance, the only British concern to use the typically Swiss mountain gauge of 800 mm. and imported locomotives, and is one of the very few steam-hauled rack railways left anywhere in the world. It can also claim to have been in virtually uninterrupted use for some 75 years, since even during the second world war it was kept working for the benefit of (and to blind spies to) such abnormal activities on the cloudy peaks of Yreryri as the development of radar.

To work some twenty return trips a day in the summer season, the line steams seven locomotives. All were built by the SLM of Winterthur, are of the 'kneeling cow' type with inclined boilers, and are perhaps strictly classifiable as 2(1)–2(1)–0Ts since on the Abt system the only driven wheels are interior pinions. Nos 2–5 date from the opening of the line in 1895 (No 1, which was named after a landowner who had opposed its building, ironically derailed herself on the opening day and was never replaced), and are named *Enid*, *Wyddfa*, *Snowdon* and *Moel Siabod*. Nos 6, 7 and 8 (*Padarn*, *Aylwin* and *Eryri*), similar but superheated and with shorter side-tanks, were delivered in 1923/4. All are painted light green.

The coaches in their present livery of red and cream appear modern, but in fact some are built on 1895 frames since from the start the SMR indulged in long bogie cars. It is true that the locomotives lack the curious *fin-de-siècle* charm of their open-cabbed Alpine contemporaries; but with all the auxiliary gear which they require for safe downhill running they hold a good deal of interest for the steam specialist. And such features of the line as the machinery of its points should charm any lover of the railway past.

Its scenic attractions apart, in fact, it would be a mistake to class the SMR with such lines as the Ravenglass and Eskdale (Cumb) and the Romney, Hythe & Dymchurch (Kent). Both these are longer: both have done, and continue to do, serious work for their communities and the country: and the R&E in particular has some interesting history. But these are essentially huge and beautiful models, whereas the SMR is a true railway. And it is not the least of its paradoxes that, although electrification was considered during its long planning period well before the end of the last century, it is today almost the only commercial line in Britain on which steam seems to have a reasonable future.

Such profit-orientated enterprises are anomalies on the steam-hauled railway scene, and its characteristic feature is rather the line taken over in the last twenty years—and, most likely, in the last ten or less—by an amateur group. The line itself may be an historically private one or (particularly in more recent years) an abandoned BR branch of some scenic interest where a battle against the indifference of the nationalised railways and the hostility of the Ministry of Transport has proved successful. (It should, however, be mentioned here that the National Trust has generally been sympathetic to the railway-preservation movement). Its stock may be that associated with the line for over a century—but later needing patient rebuilding—or a fairly random collection of locomotives and carriages owned by the society or individual members; and there are many other variables. Every line and society, in fact, has its own flavour.

What they have in common is that all have been made possible by a certain concatenation of capabilities—one or two men of capital, one or two experts in law, accountancy or the in-fighting of local politics, a backing from professionals in the fields of civil and mechanical engineering, a cadre of retired railway workers, preferably some distinguished patrons (bishops are particularly forthcoming and welcome), and a host of students or other young men happy to pay a few shillings a year for the privilege of devoting week-ends, evenings and vacations to the most apparently unrewarding and unglamorous of manual labour when they could be resurrecting their own aged cars. Such is the enduring fascination of the steam locomotive.

The growth of these living museums is one of the more attractive, characteristic and unsung of the minor social trends of the post-war years, and is perhaps best compared to the spread of local arts festivals. It would be a wholly admirable movement were it not accompanied by a slight element of puritan hypocrisy; for almost every officer of these societies vehemently protests that they are not 'playing trains'. They are certainly adding to the preservation scene; but the MoT (supposedly concerned with public safety, but in fact more interested in seeing that no harm is done to existing interests) makes it particularly difficult to open a line which could serve any purpose other than the exercising of locomotives and possibly the offering to the public of short return trips.

Hence the steam societies *are* playing trains, at least in the sense that the Hallé orchestra plays Mozart. But since this is both a life-enhancing and financially self-supporting activity as well as one which adds to the diversity (and tourist revenue) of Britain, and provides useful facilities for film and TV companies, it it hard to see why it needs apology. Ultimately, though, the responsibility for this somewhat tongue-in-cheek attitude must lie with the philistine approach of recent governments and their lack of a coherent transport policy.

Currently—and despite the plan of a Manchester group to re-open the Lakeside (Windermere, Cumb) branch with some twelve locomotives and other activities at Goathland on the north Yorkshire moors—the graph of new foundations appears to be flattening out and the preservation societies themselves to be settling into a necessary period of consolidation. (One of the drawbacks of their lively individualism was that few knew what others were doing before some four-fifths of their activities became consolidated through a most valuable clearing-house known as the Association of Railway Preservation Societies, of 34 Templegate Road, Leeds 15). But they remain on a first approach bewilderingly numerous, varied and fluid. They could formally be classified by gauge, history, region, object or type of ownership and constitution—for instance, as to whether the enthusiasts actually control the railway or are merely supporters of an operating company. But from an outside viewpoint, it is more useful to separate the officially passenger-carrying systems from those still awaiting their light railway orders.

Certain lines even of this latter type, having achieved operative status, welcome visiting travellers as 'day members' in return for a donation of the few shillings which a ticket (averaging around 6d/mile, single) would have cost: one can always thus defeat the attempts of legislatures to restrict human pleasure. But other societies again have not yet put their tracks in order, are still negotiating for the purchase or lease of these, or else exist to preserve specific items of stock with no very clear plans for running. Such groups are described later; but it should perhaps be mentioned here that most of the operative lines hold one or two locomotives which will probably never steam again, but that it has seemed best to deal with such static exhibits in this chapter rather than the previous one.

It should also be noted that the private preservers, though avoiding the excesses of some American counterparts, have occasionally adopted a freer attitude towards locomotive liveries and numbers than have the public ones: the numbers quoted in this chapter are for the most part those actually borne by the engines. And a final caveat must be issued to the effect that the dates of operation of lines are given here merely as an indication, and that up-to-date information can only be obtained from the addresses cited. The phrase 'summer season' includes the whole of the months from May through to August; but most lines are open for at least part of September too, and operation in April (and especially at Easter) is also common. Many societies will also arrange for stock inspection by individuals—and trips by parties—outside their published dates.

Even after so many preliminary notes the private groups do not arrange themselves in any very logical sequence. But, having already *hwyl*-ed *croeso y Cymru*, one may well remain for a while in those hills and valleys which enfold two other famous narrow-gauge lines.

The Festiniog (*sic*) railway, with its headquarters at Harbour station, Portmadoc, Merioneth, has a unique history and has already featured twice in this book. Steam-hauled for the fifty years before the outbreak of the first world war, this 1 ft. 11½ in. link between the slate quarries and main line at Blaenau Ffestiniog and the port thirteen miles away became increasingly prosperous; but a steady decline in freight followed between the wars, and the line fell into deepening decrepitude—apart from quarry traffic in Blaenau itself—from 1946 until 1954. Then it was rescued by a group of enthusiasts acquiring the company shares.

From that latter date until 1960 this fascinating route was steadily re-opened over the nine miles from the port to Dduallt beyond Tan-y-Bwlch, with imaginative help from army engineers on the final stretch. Unfortunately, from there on the old track had been drowned by a reservoir; but the company is now surmounting even this problem, and with the aid of gelignite and a new light railway order is cutting a deviation route through to Blaenau. Meanwhile, the line offers a passenger service from Easter till late October, with nearly a dozen return journeys a day in high summer.

The Festiniog line has five diesel locomotives, dating back to 1917, for service purposes, but is renowned for its steam stud (Plate 34). The twin 0-4-0 tender saddle-tanks built by George England for the introduction of steam to the line in 1863—No 1, *Princess* and No 2, *Prince*—have survived all vicissitudes; and though the former has yet to be fully restored, *Prince* can claim (if by a margin measured in months rather than years) to be Britain's oldest working steam locomotive and one of the very few in the world to have passed the century mark. Another famous pair built for (and, indeed, by) the line are the double-ended 0–4–4–0T Fairlies, No 10, *Merddin Emrys* of 1879 and No 3 of 1885. Originally No 11, *Livingstone Thompson*, the latter acquired the splendid name of *Taliesin* together with her present number. She is now more than a commoner if less than a mythical prince, being named *Earl of Merioneth* on one flank and its Cymric equivalent on the other.

Another early locomotive—*Welsh Pony* (1867), an enlarged version of the *Prince* class and also by England—is preserved but not yet in active service; and fragments of No 4, *Palmerston*, also survive. Of engines foreign to the line another pair of twins, *Linda* and *Blanche*, are 0–4–0STs built in 1893 for the Penrhyn quarry railway. It may perhaps be mentioned here that a predecessor of this class, *Charles*, is preserved at Penrhyn Castle, and that in addition no fewer than nine narrow-gauge Hunslet 0–4–0STs built for local quarries from 1886 onwards are in private hands; in particular Bressingham Hall works *Gwynedd* and some contemporary stock, as well as a later and much rebuilt engine.

There is also an ex-WD Alco 2–6–2T of 1917 which has neither number nor, for the moment, name. Finally, the Festiniog has awaiting repair a Peckett saddle-tank and No K1, an 0–4–4–0 Beyer Garratt constructed for the Tasmanian railways. The latter—one of the first two products of its type—is also one of the only two survivors in Britain from this builder of articulated locomotives, the other—*William Francis*—being in the Bressingham Hall collection.

In addition to modern passenger carriages there are eight four-wheeled and nine bogie coaches surviving from the original stock of the Festiniog railway: most of these date back to the 1860s but have been rebuilt to various degrees. The line has also two coaches off the Welsh Highland railway and one—now used as a buffet car—from the Lynton and Barnstaple; and it owns some 170 goods vehicles, including many built for the slate traffic, now in a maroon livery. The locomotive livery is dark green and black with red lining: that of the passenger stock is at present rather more fluid.

Whilst in Yreryri it should be mentioned that the Festiniog's neighbour, which incorporated earlier quarry-lines and which for a brief fifteen years went under the title of the Welsh Highland railway, also has a supporters' group (with headquarters at Kinnerley, Radnor). This now holds—in good order after many excursions—a 1 ft. 11½ in. 2–6–2T built by Hunslet in 1906 which was for a while the Festiniog's No 12 and is christened *Russell*.

Some forty miles down the coast, the Wharf station at Towyn, which has already been mentioned as the home of a narrow-gauge museum, is also the railhead of the fourth of the steam-worked railways of north Wales. This is the Talyllyn (Plate 33), the hyphens official to the lake having been dropped by the railway. Another slateworks line which became famous for its scenic attractions, this has an operating length of just under seven miles and the unusual gauge of 2 ft. 3 in.

The railway was opened in 1866, structures from this period which survive including a substantial viaduct near Dolgoch, slate station houses, sheds at Towyn (Pendre), and buildings at the lower terminus. When commercial traffic ceased in 1950 a preservation society immediately took over, so that the Talyllyn is not only the oldest of the new generation of private railways but the only one which can say "we never closed"!

Again the survivors—which represent the entire original locomotive stud—form a pair of sisters, though in this case not twins since *Talyllyn* is an 0–4–2ST of 1864 (a year junior to the Festiniog's *Prince*) and *Dolgoch*, an 0–4–0 'patent' well tank of 1866: both are by Fletcher, Jennings. They have been augmented by *Sir Haydn* (1878), an 0–4–2ST built by H. Hughes for the Corris railway, which carried the same number under four ownerships including that of BR, and *Edward Thomas*, a Kerr Stuart of the same notation and provenance but built in 1921 and now fitted with a Giesl ejector. These carry the numbers 1–4 respectively. The steam stock is completed by No 6 *Douglas*, a gadgetty ex-RAF Barclay 0–4–0WT of 1918. No 5, *Midlander*, is a Ruston Hornsby diesel.

The entire original stock of five four-wheeler carriages also survives, most of these having been built by the company of Brown Marshall which supplied the Festiniog railway too. A dozen other passenger carriages include several of antiquity from other Welsh narrow-gauge lines such as the Corris (which now also has a supporters' group of its own) and the Glyn Valley: these carry their traditional colours and, indeed, original transfers. The Talyllyn's own coaching livery is brown with red panels and green lining-out, the locomotives being dark green lined in black and yellow.

A small stock of wagons includes examples from the original slate-carrying days and from the Corris railway. Talyllyn services—basically of three trains daily—run from June to September, with a more fitful extension at the spring end of the season.

A transition towards England and the standard gauge is provided by the Welshpool and Llanfair railway. The successor of another system mentioned earlier in this book, this was opened in its present form in the same year and as a result of the same light railway Act as gave birth to the Vale of Rheidol line, and now runs for eight miles (some of them roadside) from Welshpool (Montgomery) to Llanfair Caereinion. It employs another unusual gauge, 2 ft. 6½ in.

This line (which was operated by BR for freight until 1956, and was taken over by a private society after a gap of some years) again relies upon a pair of twins for its regular steam motive-power: in this case they are Nos 1 and 2, *The Earl* and *Countess* (*sic*), both built by Beyer, Peacock as conventional 0–6–0Ts in 1902. Restored to the livery of the Cambrian railway, they work the usual type of summer service—daily in high season—through the rolling country of the Marches. Also preserved on the W&L are some coaches from the Austrian Zillertalbahn: an 0–6–0 diesel: *Nutty*, a vertical-boilered 0–4–0 Sentinel of 1929: and—probably the only representative of a type always rare in Britain—an 0–4–0+0–4–0 Mallett built by Bagnalls as recently as 1953.

Of the English standard-gauge societies, first place must be given to the Middleton Railway Trust. This, in addition to the short but historic remnant of track mentioned earlier, holds nine steam locomotives (Plate 35). Also on its list are a Hunslet diesel shunter of 1932—*John Alcock*, claimed to be the first to work on a British main line, another Hunslet, *John Courage*, and a Fowler diesel.

This group, which commenced active life in 1960, has the support of the University of Leeds (though enquiries should go to 12, Trelawn Crescent, Leeds 6), the backing of several factories alongside its tracks, and an access-point in Moor Road. It is not only the oldest of the present generation of standard-gauge private railways, but unique in that from its start it looked for useful revenue from freight rather than passenger operation: passenger tickets, in fact, are still not sold. In the event, it has regularly exchanged some 9,000 tons of goods with BR every year.

One train—usually diesel-hauled—works most afternoons in the year. The steam locomotives are stabled on private property; but the first Saturday in each summer month is an open afternoon and the first in September a 'gala' one. Then, in particular, there is little difficulty in sharing the experience of that Tsar of Russia who nearly two centuries ago 'observed the working of the line with curious interest and expressions of no slight admiration'.

Locomotives currently steamable include: the NER's class H No 1310 of 1891, an 0–4–0T designed by Edward Fletcher of which another example survives: *Windle*, an ex-glassworks 0–4–0WT built by Borrows in 1909: *Henry de Lacy II*, a classily-named—and rather classy-looking—oil-burning 0–4–0ST which came from the local builders of Hudswell, Clark in 1917 (a sister-locomotive to this is also preserved): a geared 0–4–0 Sentinel yard shunter of 1933, No 54, which was one of the Y1 class designed to answer the challenge of the internal combustion engine: and—the pride of the fleet, though due for repair—*The Great Marquess*. This final, privately-owned locomotive was built in 1938 for the LNER's West Highland line: the last of Gresley's K4 class of 2–6–0s, she is numbered 3442. *Swansea*, an 0–6–0 by Avonside of 1909 who spent some of her life on the Mumbles tramway, is preserved as a static exhibit.

The MRT also runs a Bagnall 0–4–0ST of 1953 now christened *Matthew Murray*, freight rolling-stock, and one passenger coach—No 2 from the Swansea and Mumbles line. Other exhibits include a steam crane which is claimed to be the only vehicle built for the broad gauge still in working order. Another steam locomotive—the GER's N7 0–6–2T, No 999, built in 1923—is at present in store.

The Bluebell Railway, with its headquarters at Sheffield Park station, Sussex, also operates an eclectic group of standard-gauge locomotives. Its track consists of some five miles rescued from a comparatively lightly-engineered branch which was built by the LBSCR in the 1880s as part of a new through-route to Brighton but soon relapsed into so sleepy a back-

PLATE 33

Scenes on the Talyllyn Railway. (Above) the staff is exchanged at Brynglas between trains hauled by *Talyllyn* and, with ejector chimney, *Edward Thomas*: (left) *Douglas* takes water at Dolgoch.

PLATE 34

Some of the Festiniog line's historic locomotives—(above left) *Linda* waiting at Tan-y-bwlch, (above right) a double-ended Fairlie opening a higher section of the line, and (below) *Prince* heading a works' train.

PLATE 35

Working engines on the Middleton Railway, Leeds. (Above) shows *The Great Marquess* taking a special across Bishop Auckland viaduct: *Windle* (right), and (right below) a double-heading by *Matthew Murray* and the octogenarian No 1310.

PLATE 36

These examples of the Keighley & Worth Valley line's outstanding collection of locomotives include: (above) No 4744—with condenser pipes—approaching Oxenhope: (left) Nos 1999 and 2226 double-heading outside Keighley: and (below) No 1247 near Haworth

PLATE 37

A brief selection from the engines of other preservation societies comprises: The Bluebell Railway's *Stepney* hauling an 'Ashbury' coach set (above left), the GWR's No 4555 working at Buckfastleigh in the Dart Valley (above right), *Henry Cort* running light on the Foxfield railway (right), and the Scottish RPS's ex-Caledonian No 419, now awaiting new steaming powers (below).

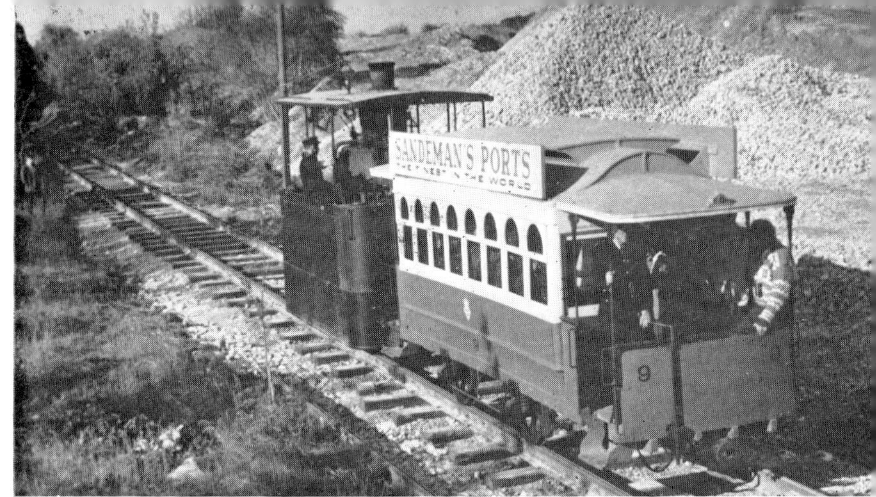

PLATE 38

Some eccentricities. Above, *George Henry*, a vertical-boilered engine built for the Penrhyn Railway by a local marine company and now preserved at the narrow gauge museum, Towyn, North Wales. Top: Britain's only working steam-tram engine, *John Bull*, patriotically hauling a Portuguese trailer on the Crick tramway, Derbyshire. Below, two turn-of-the-century motor-cars of Volk's electric railway are seen crossing on Brighton front.

PLATE 39

Industrial users of steam still include the LTB with its typical ex-GWR pannier tanks operating near Neasden (above) and—the largest of all—the NCB with similar motive power in South Wales (below).

PLATE 40

The royal luxury of Queen Victoria's LNWR saloon of 1869 (left) preserved at Clapham, and the stockbrokers' comfort of the Brighton Belle which still preserves a blend of Edwardian and jazz-age motifs (below). An epilogue on all outlived rolling stock—and, for railway addicts, a mystery picture with a built-in clue—is provided by the bottom picture.

water that the SR left it unelectrified. It was, however, renowned for the prettiness of its run through the woodlands of the Weald. And so the section beyond Horsted Keynes, closed by BR in 1958, was taken over by enthusiasts with the idea of setting up a live-steam museum, reasonably accessible to London, which should reflect primarily the LBSCR and secondarily other components of the SR—and, indeed, of the railways of the south in general.

The line, though now isolated from rail connections, has established itself with the public thanks largely to imaginative publicity. Afternoon trains are run every week-end except in deep mid-winter (but with Christmas specials): at the height of the season there is almost continuous working in daylight every day: and the engine-shed and station (where there is a museum of small exhibits) at Sheffield Park are open every day of the year in working hours.

The Bluebell line owns a petrol locomotive used only for works purposes, an ex-cement-works Aveling and Porter flywheel engine—*The Blue Circle*—built in 1926 to a pattern almost unchanged for sixty years and which was itself virtually a rail adaptation of a steam road-roller, and *Baxter*, an industrial 0–4–0T of 1877 no longer steamable. But the centre of attraction is naturally the collection of working locomotives from the south coast companies.

With its stress on the LBSCR, the Bluebell preserves two of those aristocrats of 0–6–0Ts, Stroudley's A1X class which often saw service on the line. No 72, *Fenchurch* of 1872, which after a chequered career is now the oldest standard-gauge locomotive in steam in Britain (as well as the first of her class) has been restored to the famous 'improved engine green' livery, but not her younger (by three years) sister No 55, *Stepney* (Plate 37). A later and larger LBSC engine, wearing the umber livery of her period, is No 473, *Birch Grove*, an 0–6–2T of the E4 class designed by R. J. Billinton and built in 1898.

The South-Eastern and Chatham sub-group is represented at Sheffield Park by two of Wainwright's rather unsuccessful class P 0–6–0Ts. Both were built in 1908; but whilst the non-anonymous No 27 has been restored to her elaborate original livery, No 323 has been renamed *Bluebell* and wears the line's own colour. From another south-of-the-Thames company came No 488, designed by the versatile Londoner William Adams and built by Neilsons in 1885: a 4–4–2T of the tough 415 class, she saw 75 years service before joining the Bluebell line, where she continues to add to her total of well over 1,600,000 miles in steam.

Of companies slightly more foreign to the area, the GWR has contributed No 3217 *Earl of Berkeley*, who should not be confused with the "Castle" of the same name since she is a tender 4–4–0 of Collett's hybrid "Dukedog" class. The line's stud is completed by No 2650 of 1880, the last of a class of 0–6–0Ts built to J. C. Parks' design for the LNWR's North London line, but one who passed a good deal of her life in the unlikely surroundings of the High Peak.

Bluebell rolling-stock is equally varied, the most notable exhibits being an LNWR observation coach (the only such survivor) of 1913 and a directors' saloon built for the LBSCR the following year. Other passenger stock includes examples dating back to 1894—and mainly restored to their original liveries—from the LSWR, the LCDR, the SECR (including a 'birdcage' brake) and the 'Met': the 'Ashbury' coaches from the latter, built in the closing years of the last century, are probably the oldest standard-gauge ones in regular use. There are also a number of post-amalgamation coaches from the SR, including a restaurant-car set. Freight stock comes from the southern companies (with the LBSCR contributing an interesting milk van) and the LMS.

Another society operating over an ex-BR branch, but which has only recently begun public operation, has a particularly large and representative locomotive stud. This is the Keighley and Worth Valley (enquiries to the secretary at May Bank, Fairfield, Hebden Bridge, Yorks) which runs steeply up towards the moorlands for just under five miles from Keighley station, through the tourist village of Haworth which houses—fittingly, since Bramwell Bronte once served as a ticket clerk—the railway's museum, to Oxenhope. Services at present consist of some half-dozen trains every Saturday and Sunday in summer.

The oldest KWVR locomotive currently operative dates back to 1880: this is Johnson's half-cab 0–6–0T which later bore the LMS No 1708 but is virtually as built apart from her firebox. There follows the Lancashire and Yorkshire's No 957, built by Beyer, Peacock in 1887, and an example of Barton Wright's class 25 or "Ironclad" 0–6–0s. *Sir Berkeley* is an industrial 0–6–0 with a tower-like saddle tank and open footplate constructed by Manning, Wardle in 1891. The second of the main-line companies in which the KWVR is particularly interested, the Great Northern, is first represented by its No 1247, an Ivatt 313 (later J52) 0–6–0ST of 1897.

From the start of the present century came two of Aspinall's neat little L&Y class 21 0–4–0STs nicknamed Pugs: originally numbered 68 and 19 (BR No 51218 and LMS No 11243 respectively), these were built in 1901 and 1910, again respectively. The provenance of another pair of locomotives was the largest private railway system in Britain, that of the Manchester Ship Canal. Of these Hudswell, Clarke 0–6–0Ts, No 31 was built in 1903 and No 67, though almost identical save for a prolongation of the tanks which spoils her looks, in 1919.

The LNER's N2 No 4744 also dates back to the GNR era, being built in 1921: an 0–6–2T with Gresley's touch apparent, she is notable for the condenser pipes fitted for her use in that railway anomaly of London, the long Moorgate tunnel. 1926 saw the building of No 13000, the first 2–6–0 of Hughes' class 5 "Crabs" which were also the first engines of LMS design. An interesting locomotive which links L&Y features to the high running-plates of the last age of steam, she is loaned to the KWVR from the BR collection. No 1973 is a large Avonside 0–4–0ST of the next year.

More recent engines include an 0–4–0ST of 1941, No 1999, and the SR's 0–6–0T No 30072 which was acquired as a heritage of wartime lease-lend: built by the Vulcan Ironworks of the USA in 1943, her appearance is unmistakably transatlantic. A sister to this engine is privately preserved elsewhere. Another KWVR industrial 0–4–0ST is ICI's No 2226. And one of the most remarkable locomotive types ever built is represented by an 0–6–0T now christened (for family reasons) *Joem*; for these neat but humble and slightly-dated E1s or 372s were designed for the NER by Wilson Worsdell in the last century and reproduced by not only the LNER but BR too.

*Joem*, in fact, bears the BR number 69023 and was constructed in 1951, more than half a century after the first of her almost-identical sisters. A shorter time-span between design and production is represented by the good-looking 2–6–2T which carries the BR number 41241; for she was built in 1949 to an Ivatt class 2 design of three years before. Finally, *Fred* is a J94 0–6–0ST built in 1945 and modified for gasworks service.

Three locomotives are currently under repair. These are the L&Y's No 752 (and the LMS's No 11456), originally a sister to No 957 but rebuilt as a class 23 saddle-tank: the LMS No 3924, an 0–6–0 of 1920: and *Lord Mayor*, a little industrial 0–4–0ST built by Hudswell, Clarke in 1893 and on loan from the Middleton railway. And, finally, there are two important locomotives requiring more extensive rebuilding but which in time will join the steaming list. These are *Bellerophon*, an 0–6–0WT constructed by a private builder in 1874 and of such splendidly 'period' looks that one hopes she will see her hundredth birthday in steam and the LMS No 6115, *Scots Guardsman*. The latter, a (rebuilt) 4–6–0 of Fowler's noble "Royal Scot" class of 1927, is of course the line's largest locomotive and must become its flagship.

The KWVR also operates two Waggon und Maschinenbau railbuses built in 1958 and used for commuter services in the valley, a diesel-electric shunter (which was designed for comparison with a similar diesel-hydraulic), and some twenty very varied passenger coaches, not all of which are yet in service. These date from 1870 onwards and include an observation car from the *Coronation* stock of 1937, a buffet car from the *Flying Scotsman* rake of the next year, and two Pullmans including *Zena*, a first-class saloon from the GWR. Other coaches are more suburban in origin but no less important historically.

The main achievement of the KWVR, however, must lie in its locomotive stud. No fewer than 22 standard-gauge engines have been assembled there by various societies and individuals as well as the company itself—more, that is, than can be found in any museum including Clapham: all but five of them are steamable: and those five are being brought up to standard. With the rolling-stock added on, it all adds up to a very remarkable show-case for the amateur preservation movement (Plate 36).

The most recently opened of all private lines is in a somewhat different class and might equally well have been mentioned at the beginning of this chapter; for despite its support by an enthusiasts' association it is operated by a private, profit-making company. This is the Dart Valley railway, which runs for nine miles from a point near Totnes (Devon), through Buckfastleigh, where the stock is stabled and there is a small museum, to Ashburton station. There are half a dozen trains every day in the summer season.

The line is entirely devoted to GWR practice and all stock has been restored to GWR livery of the 1933 era—though with an overlay of the railway's own blazon. The oldest (and largest) of its eight unnamed locomotives is one of Churchward's heavy 2–6–2 tanks, No 4555 of 1924 (Plate 37). Two of the attractive class 48 0–4–2Ts (Nos 1420 and 1450—another of this class is privately preserved) and three class 64 0–6–0PTs, Nos 6412, 6430 and 6435, represent the 'auto train' engines built between 1923 and 1937. There is also a "Weymouth Docks" 0–6–0PT of 1934 and another 0–6–0PT, No 1638, built after nationalisation in 1951.

The DVR passenger stock includes a four-wheeler which was probably built in 1890, three engineers' saloons from the turn of the century, and Churchward's pioneering dynamometer car of 1901. There are eight more modern and conventional coaches, largely built for push-pull working. But public interest is likely to centre more on two special groups of carriages.

These are the pair of superbly-fitted 'super-saloons' which were built by Collett in 1931/32 and used on first the Plymouth boat trains and later the Newbury race specials (No 9111, *King George* and No 9116, *Duchess of York*), and a trio of Pullmans. Two of these—*Ibis*, and No 54—were built in 1923 and 1925 respectively; the last of the series is an observation car from the *Devon Belle*, rebuilt in 1947.

Also in western England, the charming small town of Bridgnorth, Salop, is the headquarters of the Severn Valley railway, whose society has also restored its gabled station of the 1860s to GWR livery. This hopes eventually for a light railway order allowing passenger services for the twelve miles south to Bewdley. At present, however, there is only occasional working at summer week-ends over the first five miles of track.

The two mixed-traffic locomotives operated by the society itself are comparatively modern, No 3205 being an 0–6–0 of Collett's 2251 class built for the GWR in 1946 and No 46443 a class 2 2–6–0 constructed by BR to Ivatt's LMS design in 1950. In addition there are under repair two 0–6–2STs—the GWR's No 813 which was built for the Port Talbot railway as its No 26 in 1901, and a Manning Wardle industrial engine of 1926—and another 0–6–0, an LMS 3F or "Jinty" tank, No 7383, dating from 1926. These are to be joined by No 48773 of Stanier's class 8F 2–8–0s (1940), and by No 43016, a class 4 2–6–0 of 1951.

The SVR also plays host to an ex-GWR diesel railcar, No 22, built in 1941. Its conventional coaching stock too is of GWR origin, the most elegant exhibit being another of the Plymouth boat-train saloons, No 1471, *Prince of Wales*. (Two more of these are privately housed at Didcot and occasionally run on the Wallingford branch with 0–4–2 No 1466 and a matching coach). Other passenger coaches, including one used as a buffet-car, date back to 1921; and the society's oldest goods wagon was built in 1890.

A line whose history has so far been unfortunate is the Kent and East Sussex, or Rother Valley, railway. The last survivor of the 'Colonel Stephens' group, and, until a few years ago fitfully worked by BR, this 13-mile route across the wealden country between Headcorn (Kent) and Robertsbridge (Sussex) differs from most other standard-gauge 'society' railways in two respects: its level country and light engineering—for it is another example of the lines begotten by the relaxing Acts of the end of the last century—made for a large number of level crossings, and if opened to passengers it would compete seriously with existing bus services. Both these facts have hitherto militated against its applications for a light railway order.

Whilst awaiting its green light and fending-off BR's designs to sell the line for scrap, the K&ESR has prepared for service three main-line locomotives. Two are from the most widely preserved of all Britain's locomotive types, the A1X LBSCR "Terriers"—No 50, *Whitechapel* (1876) and No 70 of 1872 which became the Rother Valley's own No 3, *Bodiam*. The third—owned by a private trust—is an 0–4–4T built by the SECR in 1902 as what became one of the SR's class H, numbered 263.

Two locomotives often attributed to the K&ESR are in fact independently owned and privately stored: these are the only surviving SER engines, the O1 class 0–6–0 No 65 which was built to a James Stirling design in 1896 and rebuilt by Wainwright, and another Wainwright 0–6–0, No 592, built for the SECR in 1902. But the K&ESR does house as many as eleven industrial locomotives of various types, dates and builders, including some very curious specimens: of these, the 0–6–0ST *Charwelton* has been prepared for passenger service and several others are being re-equipped too. There is also a diesel locomotive and a railcar (in this case GWR No 20) of the type which even the keenest enthusiasts for steam like to have in reserve.

Passenger stock includes four vintage SR coaches, two Pullmans (Nos 184 and 185), and an ex-North London four-wheeler. Stock is housed at Tenterden and Robertsbridge stations—the former being the association's headquarters—pending what would be a very welcome addition to the group of active society-owned lines.

To complete this section of preservation societies one must travel north of the border where a group whose stock is currently in private store, but which has hopes of operating its own line in the very near future, is the Scottish Railway Preservation Society (81 Granton Road, Edinburgh 5). In addition to an electric and a diesel 0–4–0, this society holds a 3 ft. gauge 0–4–0T of 1899, two standard-gauge industrial locomotives—one, an 0–4–0WT by Hawthorns of 1861, being the oldest survivor by a Scottish builder and the other a Neilson 0–4–0ST of 1876—and two main-line engines.

These are a Matthew Holmes North British J36 0–6–0 of 1891—*Maude* or No 673, also built by Neilsons—and a Caledonian 0–4–4T of the handsome 439 class which was numbered 419 and built at St. Rollox in 1907. (Plate 37): it may also be mentioned here that an earlier NBR locomotive, a Holmes class G or "Pug" 0–4–0ST, No 42 of 1887, is privately preserved). All these engines are in, or being brought up to, working condition and their traditional liveries.

The SRPS rolling stock includes the GNoSR 'royal' saloon of 1898, a 'Caley' brake composite, and smaller coaches and wagons from the Highland, the G&SWR and other companies, the oldest dating back to about 1870. The society's miscellaneous exhibits are at present housed in the disused BR station at Murrayfield, Edinburgh.

Three smaller operating groups are particularly interested in industrial locomotives. On the standard gauge, the Foxfield Light Railway Society of Dilhorne, Stoke, Staffs., runs a five-mile track over which it steams two 0–4–0Ts on the first Sunday in each month: these are *Henry Cort*, by Pecketts of 1903 (Plate 37), and another by Hawthorn, Leslie of 1924. This society also owns a diesel engine and one passenger coach.

Bressingham Hall, Norfolk has short tracks for the standard gauge (with an 0–6–0T as well as the two main-liners already mentioned) and metre gauge (with *Banshee*, an 0–6–0T of 1934); a 1½-mile system on the 1 ft. 11½ in. gauge is operated with a Hunslet 0–4–0ST *George Sholto* (1909), as well as the slateworks engines mentioned above (Plate 32). The museum, which also houses a large number of steam tractors, is open on Sundays in high summer.

And finally, the rector of Cadeby, near Nuneaton has laid in his grounds a hundred yards of 2 ft. gauge track which provides exercise-room for *Pixie*, an 0–4–0 Bagnall quarry side-tank of 1919 (Plate 32), who is sister to one preserved at Birmingham. Two other industrial tank engines, *Sgt. Murphy*, an 0–6–0 Kerr Stuart of 1918, and *Margaret*, a Hunslet 0–4–0 of 1894, await repair. Some wagons and signals are also preserved, together with two internal-combustion locomotives.

Although steaming is normally restricted to one Saturday every month, the Rev E. R. Boston (who also owns a steam traction engine and road-roller) welcomes visits from railway enthusiasts at any reasonable time—but *not* Sunday mornings—and will direct them to a neighbouring enthusiast now building his own track for two 'industrials' nearby at Newbold Vardon. A number of other very short private lines for the working of industrial locomotives are planned elsewhere in Britain.

Also in a position intermediate between the societies and the individual owners, the artist Mr David Shepherd has formed a trust owning two BR locomotives—the class 4 4–6–0 *Green Knight* (No 75029, 1951) and the massive 9F 2–10–0 now christened *Black Prince* (No 92203, 1958). Another owner in a special position is Mr. Alan Pegler, who had the foresight to arrange a long-term operating contract with BR when he purchased Gresley's famous A3 (rebuilt from A1) Pacific No 4472 of 1923, *Flying Scotsman*. This contract has still some years to run: and for that time, at least, a solitary representative of steam may still be seen from time to time above the inhospitable nationalised metals (Plate 25).

Another Gresley Pacific enthusiast is the Scottish laird, Mr. James Cameron, who found himself in the fortunate position of owning land in Fife which surrounded the former Lochty station. From this he, and a like-minded group, have built a mile and a half of new track—including main-line features—to exercise A4 No 4488, *Union of South Africa*, built (as her now-sad name suggests) in the better days of 1937. She is accompanied by an observation car, No 7019, and operates on Sundays in high summer. Three more of this glamorous—but perhaps over-preserved—group, however, are for the moment immobile: these are No 4498, also built in 1937 and now bearing the name of her distinguished designer, *Sir Nigel Gresley*

(Plate 25); No 4489 *Dominion of Canada*; and No 4464 *Bittern.* An A2 Pacific built under nationalisation in 1948—*Blue Peter*, No 60532—is also privately preserved, as is the B1 4–6–0 No 61306 of the same year.

Most of the societies and even individuals mentioned above are fortunate in having their own tracks, *in esse* or *in posse.* For when the withdrawal of steam from BR became imminent, the nationalised body was disposing of superfluous stock cheap: a shunter might then cost little more than a good second-hand car, and for the price of a Jaguar you could have owned one of the noblest machines ever built. Furthermore, there appeared a reasonable future for steam-hauled specials on BR metals, whether behind the railways' own preserved engines or those rescued by private enthusiasts.

In the middle of the last decade this decision—like so many BR decisions—was reversed, and it was announced that steam would be banned from the nationalised system. The technical reasons given were rather unconvincing: the loss of goodwill (and of revenue) was clear: a breach of faith was at least arguable. But the result was that perhaps fifty privately-owned locomotives were left like stranded whales in scattered running-sheds.

Since then, some have been moved (with, of course, a diesel in costly and unneeded attendance) to the private lines. But capacity here is limited, and the majority await either another reversal of policy or the opening of further private tracks of the type which are in any case not really suitable for main-line passenger engines. The storage situation would, however, be considerably more critical were it not for the good offices of the Longmoor Military railway which houses—for instance—David Shepherd's two locomotives and the 0–4–0WT, *Lord Fisher* (No 125 of 1915).

This unique system runs for some 11 miles north from Liss, Hants. Originally an adjunct of the Royal Engineers, and now of the Royal Corps of Transport, it was set up to train army engineers in the arts of building, operating—and demolishing—military lines. Helping this task are the establishment's own 2–10–0 (No 600 *Gordon*, of 1943, the first British-built engine of this notation and a precursor of the BR 9F class) and an 0–6–0ST of 1953, No 196 or *Errol Lonsdale*, which like a disused sister belongs to the LNER's J94 class.

But Longmoor has an unexpected interest in preservation too. And in addition to a museum of military transport in general, it houses two interesting static locomotives the loveable toy-like 0–4–0WT *Gazelle* which was built in 1893 and saw service in the second world war (but who is best remembered for her work as the ill-fated Shropshire and Montgomeryshire railway's No 1), and *Woolmer*, an 0–6–0ST built by Avonside for the War Department as No 74 in 1910.

Furthermore, in recent years this line has not only played temporary host to six privately-preserved engines—including some massive passenger express locomotives—but has offered facilities for their overhaul and steaming. All that is to be regretted is that by the nature of this somewhat-secretive establishment public access is very limited, being normally restricted to one open Saturday every summer and a few other days when arrangements are made for parties.

The owners of the locomotives which have so often been left high and dry divide into several classes. Taking first the societies formed on a regional basis, the Midland and Great Northern Joint Railway Preservation Society, with headquarters at Sheringham (Norfolk) station, has two Great Eastern steam engines in addition to a pair of Waggon und Maschinenbau diesel railbuses of 1958, and coaching stock including a rake of four of Gresley's LNER articulated type of 1924. These engines are an 0–6–0 of the large J15 class, No 564 built in 1912, and a B12 4–6–0, based on Holden's distinguished design, which was in fact built by Beyer Peacock after the amalgamation in 1928. An associated body is now hoping to open the three miles of track to Weybourne.

The North-Eastern Locomotive Preservation Group is reported to own the J27 0–6–0 No 65894 and the Q6 0–8–0 No 63395. The London Railway Preservation Society (8 High Stile, Dunmow, Essex), too, has two main-line locomotives, a 2–4–0 by Beattie for the LSWR of 1874 (original No 314 and BR 30585) which is the twin of one in the BRB collection, and the Metropolitan railway's second No 1 (LTE No L44), an E class 0–4–4T designed by T. F. Clark and built in 1896. This society and its members also own seven industrial locomotives dating back to 1891—mainly 0–4–0STs by Bagnall, Barclay and Hunslet, but with an interesting flywheel Aveling and Porter—and coaching stock including an LNWR diner of 1905 and a LCDR four-wheeler of 1885.

Finally, the (Midlands) Railway Preservation Society (14 Highdale Drive, Little Haywood, Staffs) also has plans for operating regular services. Meanwhile it has collected a wide range of stock. Its only main-line engine is, rather unexpectedly, one of Stroudley's class E 0–6–0Ts, which began life in 1877 as No 110, *Burgundy*, but later worked on a colliery line under her present name of *Cannock Wood*. But she is backed up by eleven industrial locomotives, including a Neilson of 1882 and five others dating from before 1914.

Passenger rolling-stock stored by this society includes five nineteenth-century coaches built for as many different systems (most of which owe their survival to later use on such private railways as the Derwent Valley), an LNWR postal van of 1909, and the Midland's royal saloon of 1912—both of these being loaned by the BRB. There are also some goods wagons and cranes dating back to the 1880s, and a range of smaller exhibits such as signals.

A somewhat different type of society exists for the maintenance—and, when possible, steaming—of particular locomotives: these groups are often named after their sole engine or its class. From the Southern railway, for instance, came BR No 35028, *Clan Line* (a "Merchant Navy" rebuilt from her 1948 state), and another and lighter Bulleid 4–6–2, the "West Country" *Blackmore Vale* of 1946 originally numbered 123 and remaining in her original airsmoothed condition. Though belonging to different societies, both these are stabled at Longmoor. Also housed there is No 41298, an Ivatt 2–6–2T of 1951 similar to one used on the Keighley and Worth Valley line.

The LMS Pacific No 6201, *Princess Elizabeth*, recalls by her name the distant days of 1933 when Her Majesty was in the Brownies. A long-distance record-holder in her time, she is now stored together with a slightly earlier coach from the BR collection. Also privately preserved in steamable condition are two Stanier "Jubilee" 4–6–0s of 1934, Nos 5593, *Kolhapur* and 5596, *Bahamas*.

Storage, too, is the present fate of a group of GWR locomotives owned privately or by the Great Western Society. These include two "Castles"—Messrs. Gretton and McAlpine's No 4079 *Pendennis Castle* of 1924, and Mr. P. B. Whitehouse's No 7029, *Clun Castle*—and the smaller 4–6–0 No 6998, *Burton Agnes Hall* of 1949. (As Hamilton Ellis has pointed out, the GWR ran very short of names for this huge class, though they did not quite descend to *Dotheboys Hall*). In the same group are *Cookham Manor*, No 7808 (1938): a 2–6–2T, No 6106, of 1931; the 0–6–2T No 6697 of 1928: and examples of several varieties, dating from 1934 onwards, of the popular 0–6–0PTs.

A final miscellany of preserved locomotives would take in a number of cases where owners have deliberately avoided publicity (at least whilst discussing storage arrangements with BR) or consider future plans so uncertain that no useful information can be given. This list includes the interesting GER 0–4–0ST No 10229 of 1870: the L&Y 0–6–0 No 1300 (misnumbered 1122) of 1896: the NER's unusual 0–8–0 No 2238 of 1918: the LNER's 0–4–0T No 985 and 0–6–0T No 5894 (both in 1923): the LMS 4–6–0 No 5428 (1937): and two BR engines to LMS design, 2–6–0 No 46411 (1950) and 4–6–0 No 43106 (1951). At least three more locomotives were the subject of fund-raising activities as this book went to press.

Over 160 steam locomotives—most of them in working order—have been mentioned above, and form a larger (if not more important) group than those in the public, static collections. But even were the list complete (and the continually-revised stock-books from which it has been compiled must themselves confess to areas of doubt and the need for stop-press amendments), it would still not fully represent the survival of steam in Britain.

The industrial locomotive—steam, diesel or even electric—is not quite a breed of its own, for some of the more interesting engines mentioned above owe their survival to the fact that, after having been sold off by their main-line owners, they entered a new life in some colliery or steelworks: there they endured, whilst the rest of their class were broken up, to enter the present age of preservation. In addition, several dozen more purely industrial or contractors' locomotives have crept into the foregoing discussions.

Until a few years back, perhaps, interest in these little 0–4–0 and 0–6–0STs was largely confined to a group of enthusiasts with their own Industrial Locomotive Preservation Society ("Channings", Kettlewell Hill, Woking, Surrey) and several regional groups. But with the passing of steam and the great upsurge of interest in all forms of railway objects, when even a bedroom utensil can change hands for over £5 if it bears the arms of a Victorian company, the 'industrials' have entered into their own. Needless to say, their cheapness—at around £100 in working order—has not detracted from their popularity with the individual collector who may also see a chance of capital appreciation. But a number too have been sentimentally preserved by their original owners.

Several locomotives not already mentioned are of unusual interest in this group, such as the Head, Wrightson vertical-boilered 'coffee pots' built in the 1860s: at least three of these survive, of which one is destined for public display. The Penrhyn Castle museum in Caernarvon has a particularly good collection of industrials as well as of rolling stock from the neighbouring slate railways, its exhibits including a gasworks 0–4–0WT of 1870 and a 3 ft. gauge 0–4–0ST of 1882. Another Victorian 0–4–0ST, the ex-GWR *Trojan* (1897), is privately held. But there can be found preserved (and usually open to inspection where not actually on exhibition) some twenty or thirty other industrial engines of various degrees of antiquity and charm at sites ranging from Knock in Banff to Lee Moor in Devon by way of Kidderminster, Droitwich and Leighton Buzzard. One of the largest private collections, some of whose ten members are destined to steam at Windermere, is at Lytham St Annes, Lancs.

To illustrate the very varied fates of industrial locomotives, one need consider only the present state of a delightfully-named quartet of cement-works 0–6–0STs built in the early years of the present century. Of these, *Triassic* is statically tended by a private owner, *Jurassic* is steamed on a seaside pleasure-line near Grimsby, *Mesozoic* sits in a breaker's yard and *Liassic* is in Canada. This book can hence make no pretence of offering a complete catalogue of the "industrials".

Live steam is fading from active factory railways almost as fast as it has from the main-line system, though this may be a place to mention that one unexpected user—not strictly classifiable as industrial, and indeed now claiming to be the last employer of steam in general service—has long remained faithful to it thanks to its rather intermittent demands on locomotives. For the London Transport Board continues to employ for its nocturnal activities in the Neasden and Lillie Bridge (West Kensington) areas a stud of eight maroon-liveried, class 74 0–6–0PTs which represent the last of the historic link between the District and Met systems and the GWR. These are now being worked into the ground, but have at least one more year of life. (Plate 39).

In a unique position, too, is the National Coal Board, which, until the last moment felt itself bound by prestige to employ steam locomotives just as British Waterways has to add to its losses by conducting uneconomic internal operations by canal transport. The NCB, in fact, still operates over four hundred engines (including representatives of every important builder of 'industrials'), divided over a score of areas and almost every active coalfield in Britain (Plate 39). It is unfortunately impossible in the confines of this book to list even the sites involved, let alone the actual locomotives: the stud is now being reduced fast, but the NCB's allegiance to steam still mocks at this attempt to catalogue the last survivors of an age·

By virtue of its intensely seasonal nature the sugar-beet industry has a use for the steam locomotive in East Anglia as much as in northern France, and in addition to final survivors on miscellaneous dock, generating station and factory systems (there are two, for instance, serving a nylon works near Grimsby and quite a few in the service of the automobile at Ford's, Austin's and Dunlop's) locomotives of comparatively heavy and modern types may continue to be used for several years yet in two other coal-based industries. These are steelworks—at least for their longer hauls out to quarries—and gasworks until a natural-gas policy is agreed.

For those who loved the passenger express in its gleaming heyday, it is perhaps sad to reflect that steam's last 'serious' work will almost certainly be carried out in the grubby service of a coal-pit which is itself doomed as uneconomic. But historically it is apt that it should be so, and a wheel has come full circle. For it was in the mines that it all began, four centuries ago.

# IX CARRIAGES AND CATERPILLARS

It is easy to think of half-a-dozen experts on the history of the steam locomotive: it is difficult to think of more than one (and he, of course, is Hamilton Ellis) on that of passenger coaches: it is impossible to name a single specialist in freight rolling-stock. This last, in fact, forms almost the least glamorous department of the railways' stock-in-trade, and such goods wagons as have been preserved have often been so as parts of 'package deals' and hence mentioned already in this book.

Passenger stock, however, is considerably more than the proverbial follower of the Lord Mayor's show of the locomotive: it forms the bulk of that classic, composite ideal, the train. And hence the preservation societies mentioned in the previous chapter have also rightly saved from the knacker's yard a handful of the splendid saloons which were the last exemplars of a century-long tradition of custom-built coaching stock, as well as representatives of mass-produced but still characteristic regional designs. Several groups, indeed, specialise in the preservation of coaches from such localised lines as the Hull & Barnsley.

Much, though, has been lost of both types. For when even the last of Britain's observation cars could be scrapped from the West Highland line with little protest or publicity it is not surprising that whole classes of more humble rolling-stock are now represented (if at all—and some detection is still possible here) only by conversions into inspection, work or camping coaches—or, with still less distinction, into wayside allotment sheds and chicken-coops.

Of the civic museums interested in transport, few have even one complete coach to exhibit; but fortunately the BRB collection is almost as representative here as on the locomotive side, with over fifty carriages and wagons on or awaiting display. The earliest have already been mentioned; and from the middle of the nineteenth century onwards such prototype specialised rolling-stock as a crane (GNR, 1850), a horse-carrying 'dandy car' (NBR, 1861), a postal sorting van (West Coast Joint Stock, 1885), an oil tanker (private, 1889), a snow plough (NER, 1891), a milk van (Metropolitan, 1896), a dynamometer car (NER, 1906) and two fire engines are represented, as well as several stages in the development of the ordinary open goods wagon.

Only one Victorian guard's or brake van (from the LSWR of 1894) has been officially preserved. But the interest of the non-specialist is in any case more likely to centre on the passenger carriages mentioned below. These are displayed—except where otherwise stated—at Clapham.

The oldest 'normal' coach—a 1/2 composite—comes from the Stockton and Darlington and is dated at around 1845: another from the next year has also survived, and these are preserved at the York museum and at Stockton station respectively. But the first fifteen years of passenger rail travel would be unrepresented were it not for three happy accidents, the first of which is that (as mentioned in an earlier chapter) the Cornish Bodmin and Wadebridge line, though in other respects a normal railway, remained stone-sleepered until almost the end of the nineteenth century. It was hence treated by the LSWR as a backwater whose stock was not in common use, so that two original coaches of 1834 served until the conventionalisation of the line after its diamond jubilee. Then, together with a composite whose body dated from about 1860 but whose frame is possibly of 1837 (now at Clapham), they were regarded as historic relics and set aside for preservation as unique survivors of their age.

These are now at York, which also preserves from the North Eastern railway the body of a carriage of 1840 of which this part alone has survived the hazards of time. (The Bristol museum has another fragment, one side of a Bristol and Exeter broad-gauge carriage of 1849). And from the London and Birmingham of 1842 comes a unique exhibit. Basically a first-class four-wheeler, it had a 'boot' opening into one of its three compartments so as to accommodate the feet of Queen Adelaide whenever it pleased William IV's dowager (a more intrepid traveller than her niece, Victoria) to assume the horizontal. It is *not* the world's first sleeper, since the same railway had public "bed-carriages" running four years earlier; but it *is* of great interest as demonstrating how much the earliest 'luxury' rail carriages owed to the tradition of stage-coach design.

The main line of carriage development is illustrated by a coach from the Eastern Counties company of 1850: from the same year comes a detached body, but both are now in store. One or two items of more doubtful provenance have also survived from this period. But for all but the specialist the mid-century years are epitomised by what is perhaps the world's most famous and magnificent railway coach, the twin saloons built by the LNWR for Queen Victoria in 1869 which were amalgamated into a single vehicle in 1895 (Plate 40). Its gilded headstocks and deeply-padded blue interior, its fretted handles, twin beds and oil lighting—for the Queen was afraid of gas—have often been described and photographed: the accommodation for the entourage (with a special room for the egregious John Brown) is hardly less ornate: and the toilet is a period piece by itself. A fragment of the GWR royal saloon of 1872, described by Hamilton Ellis as pompous rather than luscious, also survives at Clapham.

A saloon of the same year which housed the directors of the very mundane North London railway on their arduous journeys between Richmond and Broad Street provides a transition to the everyday world represented by a Midland railway six-wheeler of 1885. Now in store, this appears a recognisable step towards modernity for the ordinary traveller who was beginning to benefit from the same company's socialistic policy of giving third-class passengers second-class facilities; but it must be remembered that the first *preserved* example of almost every innovation towards increased comfort generally follows a decade or so behind its introduction in regular service on some line, which itself lags behind use in special saloons. This applies to springing, buffing and drawgear, bogies, toilets, corridor connection and air-conditioning, so that preserved rolling stock is less representative of continuous advance than are preserved locomotives.

Another six-wheeler, stored by the Bristol museum, comes from the GWR of 1887; and a further move towards present-day standards is represented by the East Coast Joint Stock's coach of 1898, also now in store. The century closes, however, with another aristocratic carriage, the private saloon of the Sutherland family which had shown such enthusiasm for railways in their earlier days. The Duke himself preferred to travel on the footplate.

The twentieth century opens with another fine vehicle from the LNWR, a royal dining car. Three years later this was joined by two slightly nautical saloons built for the newly-crowned King Edward and his wife; these, later equipped with a silver-plated bath, were to serve royalty for over forty years. The vernacular tradition is represented by coaches from the 'Met' (1900) and the LSWR (1903): both are in store. But in this new age even a grocer could travel in quasi-royal state for the price of a Pullman-car supplement on the Brighton line—in, for instance, *Topaz* of 1913. Edwardian opulence also appeared in a dining-car built in the last year of peace for the joint Scottish service of the Midland and the Glasgow and South Western railways.

The BRB collection is continued by a stored coach (1920) from the Caledonian railway and an LNER third-class sleeper of 1931; and it concludes, so far as locomotive-hauled carriages are concerned, with a final representative of custom-built stock, the GWR buffet saloon No 9631 of 1934. But the last years of the independent companies are still—just—represented by vehicles remaining in service on BR.

Since the average life of a passenger coach is only some thirty years, and loss has been accelerated by both heavy wartime use and the coming of the electric and diesel multiple-unit, such survivors are rare, for the most part pressed into service only on relief or other special trains, and not destined long to be with us. One could wish that their replacements always represented an improvement in comfort (they did not do so, for instance, on the Hook continental boat trains). And certainly more individual Pullman cars could have been preserved, though the publishers of this book retain *Malaga* of 1922—an early vehicle with 6-wheel bogies, and one associated with many royal journeys—to serve as their board-room at Shepperton, Middlesex.

For the moment, however, the Western region retains a few shuntable if not runnable ex-GWR coaches which are used mainly for filming purposes. Some pre-war sleepers are also in service there; and another veteran sleeping car (No 372) runs frequently on the Midland region, which also has several ex-LMS postal sorting vans. Six sleepers still in regular use on the East

Coast route are ex-LNER ones, three of which even date back to the Gresley period. There is also a batch of ex-LNER buffet cars still serviceable, including one in regular use on the Kings Cross/Cambridge line and two which work a turn to Cleethorpes. The Eastern region has a score of postal vehicles dating back to 1929, and some ordinary passenger composites which may see a few more seasons of service.

London Transport still operates a few sets of clerestoried stock with decorative ventilation grilles, on the District lines. But—more surprisingly—the oldest rolling-stock in regular main-line use is also that which composes the multiple-unit trains on a number of electrified systems.

With the traditional Pullman coach almost passed from the scene one thinks first of the *Brighton Belle*, now running more frequently than ever with stock built for the original electrification of the line in 1933, and since then only lightly reconditioned (Plate 40). Even at that date the cars' richness of inlaid work must have struck a slightly Edwardian note; and today it represents the last of a tradition of individual coach-building, unless that title can be extended to cover the BR 'empire woods' series which have themselves become period pieces. The *Belle* has another distinction in that it has preserved the same general schedules for nearly 40 years (with 25 more of history before electrification) and during the last war was, at 50 mph, Britain's fastest train.

There are, however, still older electric train-sets in service, for some of those on the Manchester/Altrincham line date from 1931. Other lines in the Midland region, such as those of the Wirral, also run pre-nationalisation stock.

A unique and profitable survival, too, returns one to the delightful blend of periods which is Brighton: for it was along its channel shore that, in 1883, the locally-born (and buried) pioneer, Magnus Volk, built his light electric railway—the first such in England, and one of the world's earliest. Though designed primarily as a demonstration of the advantages of electric traction, the mile-and-a-quarter-long line proved such an amenity to the foreshore that it has remained in service ever since on a gauge of (approximately) 2 ft. 8½ in. and a voltage of (equally approximately) 180v DC. Several of the present cars (Plate 38) are minimally rebuilt from the Victorian originals—the oldest being No 3 of 1897—and Volk's weatherboarded headquarters survive cut into the cliff at Paston Place. While at Brighton one can still see, at low tide, the stones which mark the course of perhaps the most extraordinary transport medium ever operated, Volk's amphibious tramway to Rottingdean of 1896.

Traces of another early electric line (1866) also survive at Ryde, IoW. The first serious attempt to run inanimate railways without steam locomotives—or, indeed, any true motive power on the train itself—dates, however, from more than 40 years earlier. This took the form of the 'atmospheric' or 'aerial' lines which worked on the principle of a piston sliding in an evacuated main laid between the trunks: conceived as early as 1801, they became popular in the late 1830s and early 1840s. Their effect on the station architecture south from Exeter has already been mentioned: a less welcome legacy of Brunel's mistake in adopting the system is to be found in the steep grading of this route beyond Newton Abbot.

Another line worked by air-power was that between London Bridge and Croydon. The only memorial to the first of its four propulsive systems (since steam and overhead-wire electrification also preceded the present third-rail supply), however, has been transported; for the railway's pumping-house at Croydon was sold to the local water authority and in 1851 re-erected in its entirety about mile a further south at Waterworks Square, Surrey Street. There—minus its tower—it still stands as part of a Jacobethan complex. Surviving specimens of the pneumatic tubing itself come from the Devon line and are to be found in the York and Swindon railway museums and that of Newcastle.

Reverting to electric traction, a selection of early locomotives, motor-cars and stock has found its way to the national transport museums. Their first serious use was of course on the London tube lines; and from the first of these, the City and South London railway which now forms part of the Northern line, an original and curious (but somewhat restored) Crompton locomotive of 1889, which is numbered '1' but was not the first to be built, is preserved in the Science Museum. This could be matched with the tubular 'padded cell' coach from the same line—famous for the fact that its windows were mere arrow-slits which looked out on the only things worth seeing underground, the station names—which is preserved at York. Part of a motor-car for the (present) Piccadilly line, which was built in Hungary in 1906, is on show at Clapham.

An early appearance of electric traction on a surface railway is commemorated by a bogie centre-cab locomotive which was fitted for both overhead and third-rail collection, built for the NER in 1904, numbered 26500 or ES1, and is now exhibited at Leicester (Stoneygate). In store at Edinburgh is a primitive-looking Baldwin/Westinghouse electric locomotive of 1902. The Shugborough Hall collection includes a somewhat mysterious battery 0–4–0 built for the North Stafford railway, and two motor-coaches have been preserved in store by the BRB: these come from the LNWR North London line (1915) and the SR suburban system (1925). Finally, the Science Museum has a typical motor-car from the Piccadilly line, built in 1927 but appearing surprisingly modern.

Even those least interested in electrified lines may feel that this selection is a thin and scattered one and regret the lack of visible representatives of (say) the Liverpool Overhead railway, whose coach No 3 of 1892 is in store for the city of Manchester. But the internal-combustion locomotive and motor-coach has suffered still worse, pioneering efforts in this field having generally been broken up by their owning companies long before it was realised that the future was largely to belong to them. In particular, one regrets that the Edwardian petrol railcar has vanished as completely as its steam counterpart, save for one Irish example.

Hence there needs to be added to the details on internal-combustion exhibits given earlier no more than notes to the effect that the Swindon collection preserves an AEC railcar, No 4, built for the GWR in 1934, and the Shugborough one a petrol shunter of 1920. The Science Museum, however, houses in lonely state the prototype 'Deltic' diesel locomotive which English Electric built in 1955 but which was never taken over by BR. The rather more historic gas-turbine No 18100 appears to be destined for scrap metal.

This book, though, cannot quite forget the urban tram. To some extent the predecessor of the conventional railway, to some extent its descendant and to some extent its rival, this belongs in a debatable territory between road and rail transport. Furthermore, steam (and, even more, internal-combustion) town trams made only a small impact on the English scene, and even less of their rolling-stock survives than of the age of horse traction.

The electric tram, though, inhabits a landscape of its own and has attracted its particular devotees, museums and literature, the central body being the Light Railway League (54 Twyford Avenue, London W.3). Only one system—that at Blackpool, Lancs—remains commercially operative, though this demonstrates that with modern equipment (and there is little antiquarian interest to this line, though it incorporates an experimental length of 'conduit' track laid in 1885) the urban tram is as viable a means of transport in Britain as it is recognised as being on the continent. But a few survive as seaside attractions; and, in addition, the dedicated tram-hunter will still find (particularly in Yorkshire and Lancashire, and perhaps confused by trolleybus traces) a host of reminders of the heyday of this form of transport in the shape of cast-iron standards, converted depots, changes in road surfaces and rails only half-tarred over.

Individual tramway and light electric railway cars are preserved in the national and regional museums with an interest in transport—for instance, at South Kensington and Birmingham—and there is also a display of about a dozen at Clapham. Unexpectedly, only four of these last come from London's transport systems; for, as has been mentioned, Clapham is an anomalous place and currently houses a number of electric trams from provincial towns as well as two horse-tramway cars. The time-span extends fairly representatively from 1883 to 1952.

An even more comprehensive display—and certainly a more exciting one—awaits those who find their way to the rather remote site of Crich in Derbyshire. There, just under a mile of an historic quarry roadbed referred to earlier has been re-railed by enthusiasts and now functions as a living museum where some 40 vehicles (predominantly from north-country systems, but with an overseas representation too) offer rides at summer week-ends. In addition to the electric stock, there is a vertical-boilered steam tram locomotive No 2, *John Bull*, by Beyer Peacock of 1885 (Plate 38). This is the only steamable one in Britain, though a rather decrepit specimen of the breed is in BR store and one from an Ulster line in the Hull museum.

But these passionate amateurs are now at work on an even more imaginative long-term scheme. It is also a somewhat paradoxical one. For instead of building a tramway to serve a community they are building a community to recapture a tram-scape, and in a deeply rural setting are re-creating the type of urban environment which was recently dismissed as dull if not disgusting. Only today indeed, with endless obscenities being scrawled on the pylon-ed, motorway-ed, skyscraper-ed wall of England, could even the Coronation Street of 1910 appears an epitome of elegance.

But this is the ambience aimed at by the Crich Tramway Museum Society (enquiries to 29 Brunswick Road, Manchester 20); and in time its officers hope to surround their terminus with a translated conservatory (as cafeteria), chapel (as exhibition hall), shops, pub and houses, as well as a range of late-Victorian and Edwardian street furniture, slot-machines and outdoor objects of *virtu*. The scheme is so much more original than any conceived by a mere *railway* preservation society that it seems to justify mention in this book, where it is only marginal to what is itself a marginal subject. It is, indeed, of transatlantic dimensions—though in typically English fashion it is based on committee-work rather than foundations, on amateur sweat rather than strokes of a benefactor's pen.

It also appears to have a keen sense of priorities. For the society has already acquired a cast-iron *pissoir*.

## *MISCELLANY*

More than any other industry, that of transport is linked to the life of the community; and more than any other form of transport, the railways in their classic age created an ambience of their own. Engineering and architectural works, locomotives and rolling stock are perhaps the objects of greatest interest on that scene; but this book cannot conclude without passing reference to a few of the thousand other types of object which can only be classified as 'railwayana.'

Many enthusiasts may feel that signalling equipment, at least, should not be so lightly dismissed; but in fact this department of railway technology has received little systematic attention by preservationists. Clapham exhibits a fairly representative selection of curiosities ranging from the days of the 'bobbies' and hand tokens onwards (a unique exhibit being one of the typical winged chairs provided for signalmen by the North Staffordshire company) and also has a few semaphore signals and posts. But far more of the latter—and a good many, of course, still remain *in situ*, though often disused and in rather recondite spots such as a back platform of Mitcham or the stations outside Grimsby—have found their way to scattered museums and private collections.

Serious attention to signalling has, however, been paid by the Swansea industrial museum (which preserves some of the GWR's early track circuiting equipment), by those of Newcastle, Liverpool and Bristol, and in particular by the Science Museum. This, in addition to housing a comprehensive range of small exhibits including those which touch on telecommunications generally, has re-erected a typical ex-GER box and installed in it working examples of three ages of equipment dating from the 1870s onwards illustrating progress in interlocking and power-actuation. These frames (which can be operated by museum officials) are linked to signals in the main exhibition hall.

Another feature of this museum is its re-creation, for contrast with a contemporary installation, of a traditional booking office; and this mention must serve to dismiss another class of railway equipment which has its own devotees. (A most respectable looking middle-aged lady, for instance, was recently observed to board a Manchester express proudly clasping an old, toggle-action, Edmundson patent ticket-dater). For the world of railwayana has neither recognised classifications nor recognisable frontiers, and in such categories as weighing machines or the sanitary equipment manufactured (probably at Leek) by companies with splendid trade-names like Adamant and Crapper it is part of the Victorian–Edwardian world as a whole. Similarly, such exhibits as machines for the dynamic balancing of wheels (Birmingham) and the metrological instruments still in use at Horwich belong as much to the history of technology as to that of railways.

It is true that the Clapham and other museums preserve many purely railway objects, ranging from Francis Webb's patent footwarmer to the head-plates of royal locomotives or a wheel-chair for conveying invalids to what was for nearly a century their fastest form of transport, as well as a rather dreary assemblage of ceremonial spades and barrows. But faced with embossed padlocks, refreshment-room cutlery and cast-iron lamp standards, the authorities have found it as hard as any of us to define just which elements of (for instance) a scene including a clock, a station barrier, a print-your-own-label machine and a W. H. Smith's facade are true railwayana. And this may be as good a reason as any to plead that the tramway enterprise of Crich should be followed by a museum which should re-create a turn-of-the-century railway scene as a whole. This should have a top-hatted curator, enamel advertisements, cast-iron grates, a faint smell from a vanished gasworks, bombazine barmaids and machines issuing platform tickets for at least a decimal penny.

If an environment can no longer perform useful work, such preservation is a whole dimension richer than any achievable in a world of glass cases and 'no smoking' notices. But meanwhile there are rumours of odd survivals in isolated sites such as a North British drinking fountain in an (abandoned) English station, the benches and clock at Ilkley, Yorks, the original mile-posts near Glasgow (Queen Street), or the 'Wirral horn' still emblazoned on CLC stations. None of these, perhaps, is so curious as the (gas? water?) pressure-gauge which perished some years back with a wing of Ambergate before it could be identified; but they hint at the wealth of minor railway relics which are rusting or crumbling away for want of a coherent survey.

The author of this book has made no pretence of original scholarship, and certainly has no right to admonish those who have worked—in field or library, and usually for love—to preserve so much of Britain's railway heritage. One may wonder, perhaps, if some of the effort put into preserving yet *another* 'Terrier', 'Black Stanier' or 'A4,' or in following the precise trace of a Welsh tramway, might not have been better devoted to cataloguing and conserving the elusive minor relics of the railway age. But to every man his taste; and writer and reader, one hopes, are united in their gratitude to those who have made available to the future the great and curious things of the past—and in their anathemas to the vaudals in seats of power.

Beaumont, Wood, Outram, Rennie, Jessop, Trevithick, Blenkinsop, Murray: the Stephensons and Brunels: Locke and Vignoles: Mocatta and Thompson, Hardwick and Pritchett, Dobson and the Cubitts: Stirling and Allen: Stroudley, Beattie and Johnson: Drummond and Ramsbottom and (if you like) Webb: Dean, Churchward and Collett: Ivatt, Fletcher and Robinson: Bulleid, Stanier and Gresley: these were famous men, and deserve to be praised by and remembered of us.

And if this exercise, which was recommended not only by Kipling but by Terence and Ecclesiasticus, is considered too unfashionable, let us at least be thankful that something of what they achieved is still before us.

## ERRATUM

The author apologises for following published sources in attributing the stations on the Newcastle and Carlisle railway (p. 64 *et seq*) to Robert Stephenson. Their designer is unknown, but was certainly *not* RS.

## ADDENDUM

In June, 1969, the army announced that the Longmoor Military Railway (p. 103) would be 'demobilised'. There are plans for its use as a working transport museum. Several other preservation schemes were announced or made progress in the summer of 1969.

# *GAZETTEER*

ALL RELICS mentioned in the book are referred to below, with the exceptions of a few sites referred to in passing or duplicated elsewhere and of one or two collections in private hands or in localities known to be very temporary.

Wherever a feature cannot be identified by a postal address, references are given. These are based on the one-inch Ordnance Survey maps and consist of a sheet number followed by the usual six-figure indication. It should be noted, however, that the Survey was never at its best in the field of industrial archaeology and that a certain amount of detail has been lost even in preparing the current, seventh series. (In particular, the evocative words 'track of old railway' are disappearing, presumably because no symbol has been found to distinguish recent closures from important early tramways). Grid references have hence been given to the feature itself when it is identifiable—if un-named—on the one-inch sheets, but otherwise to the nearest named structure or clear feature such as a farm-house or crossroads. This should in no case be more than a few hundred yards from the relic itself.

Dates cited normally relate to the completion of the feature referred to. In the cases of some tramways and early railways, however, the date of opening of the line itself (or an 'average' date if it was built over a number of years) has been chosen, and hence years quoted may differ by a year or so from those given in other sources.

Entry in this gazetteer of course, does not imply that a site is open to public inspection.

NOTE: The symbol + after a date implies that more than one relic is to be found in the same area, the year quoted referring to the earliest.

# ENGLAND

| | | | |
|---|---|---|---|
| BEDFORDSHIRE (Beds) | | | |
| BEDFORD | Midland Road | Station | 1859 |
| BERKSHIRE (Berks) | | | |
| BASILDON | 158/606790 | Bridge | 1839 |
| MAIDENHEAD | 159/901810 | Bridge | 1839 |
| MOULSFORD | 158/595847 | Bridge | 1839 |
| SONNING | 159/759743 | Cutting | 1839 |
| WINDSOR | Riverside | Station | 1850 |
| BUCKINGHAMSHIRE (Bucks) | | | |
| DENBIGH HALL | 149/853353 | Bridge | 1837 |
| WOLVERTON | 146/815422 | Viaduct | 1838 |
| CAMBRIDGESHIRE (Cambs) | | | |
| CAMBRIDGE | | Station | 1845 |
| ELY | | Station | 1846 |
| CHESHIRE (Ches) | | | |
| CHESTER | General | Station | 1847 |
| DUTTON | 109/583764 | Viaduct | 1837 |
| RUNCORN | 100/509834 | Bridge | 1863 |
| CORNWALL | | | |
| CAMBORNE | | Museum; Tramway Exhibits | |
| PENZANCE | 190/712404 | Sleepers | 1826 |
| ST BLAZEY | 186/058571 | Viaduct | c1840 |
| SALTASH | 187/435588 | Bridge | 1859 |
| CUMBERLAND (Cumb) | | | |
| BRAMPTON JUNCTION | 76/550600 | Station | 1836 |
| BRAMPTON SANDS | | Weigh-House | 1799 |
| CARLISLE | Citadel | Station | 1847 |
| | London Road | Station | 1841 |
| KIRKHOUSE AND FARLAM | 76/567589 | Earthworks | 1775 |
| MONKWRAY | 82/167969 | Earthworks | 1738 |
| WETHERAL | 76/468546 | Viaduct | 1836 |
| WHITE GILL | 82/053337 | Earthworks | 1755 |
| DERBYSHIRE (Derby) | | | |
| AMBERGATE | 111/350516 | Station | 1840+ |
| BRIER LOW | 111/076690 | Bridge | 1830 |
| BROADOAK | 111/395532 | Earthworks | c1817 |
| BUNSAL FARM | 111/017760 | Bridge | 1830 |
| BURBAGE | 111/032737 | Tunnel | 1830 |
| BUXTON | | Station | 1863 |
| CHAPEL-EN-LE-FRITH | 111/065814 | Incline | 1796 |
| CHAPEL MILTON | 111/058817 | Tunnel | 1796 |
| CRICH | 111/350544 | Inclines | 1793 |
| | | Working Tramway Museum | |
| DERBY | Friargate | Bridge | 1878 |
| | Midland Road | Station and Hotel | 1840 |
| DINTING | 102/019945 | Viaduct Remains | 1844 |
| DOVE HOLES | 111/073784 | Tunnel | 1863 |
| FERNILEE | 111/018787 | Bridge | 1830 |
| FRITCHLEY | 111/359530 | Bridges | 1793 |
| GRIVES WOOD | 112/495552 | Earthworks | 1819 |
| HIGHPEAK JUNCTION | 111/310560 | Incline, etc. | 1830 |

| | | | |
|---|---|---|---|
| HORWICH END | 111/013805 | Bridge | 1830 |
| HURDLOW | 111/127661 | Bridge | 1830 |
| LITTLE EATON | 120/364420 | Bridge | 1795 |
| MIDDLETON | 111/291555 | Incline, etc. | 1830 |
| ROWSLEY | 111/259660 | Old Station | 1849 |
| SMITHY HOUSES | 111/386471 | Track | 1795 |
| TICKNALL | 121/356238 | Bridge and Tunnels | 1802 |
| WEST HALLAM | 121/432412 | Earthworks | 1817 |
| WINGFIELD | 111/385557 | Station | 1840 |
| WOODHEAD | 102/135001 | Tunnel | 1845 |

DEVONSHIRE (Devon)

| | | | |
|---|---|---|---|
| BUCKFASTLEIGH | | Working Steam Railway | |
| DAWLISH | 188/963767 | Sea Wall | 1846 |
| EXETER | St Thomas | Station | 1846 |
| HAYTOR DOWN | 175/761778 | Granite Track | 1820 |
| LEIGHAM | 187/512585 | Tunnel | 1823 |
| NEWTON ABBOT | Station | Locomotive Preserved | |
| ROBOROUGH | 187/503622 | Earthworks | 1823 |
| STARCROSS | | Station | 1846 |
| TORRE | | Station | 1848 |

DORSETSHIRE (Dorset)

| | | | |
|---|---|---|---|
| CORFE | Wareham Road | Bridges | 1806 |
| FORTUNESWELL | 178/685722 | Sleepers | 1826 |
| POUNDBURY | 178/683912 | Tunnel | 1852 |

DURHAM, County

| | | | |
|---|---|---|---|
| BISHOPSWEARMOUTH | Cemetery | Bridge | 1813 |
| BRUSSELTON | 85/195255 | Incline and Sleepers | 1825 |
| BYERMOOR | 78/184572 | Earthworks | 1712+ |
| CONSETT | 84/096490 | Viaduct | 1858 |
| CRAWCROOK | 78/135635 | Earthworks | 1663 |
| DARLINGTON | Bank Top Station | Locos Preserved | |
| | North Road | Station | 1842 |
| FATFIELD | 78/308538 | Earthworks | 1710 |
| GATESHEAD | | Station | 1841 |
| HETTON-LE-HOLE | 85/357473 | Tunnel | 1828 |
| HIGH SPEN | 78/137596 | Earthworks | 1708 |
| LOW ETHERLEY | 85/170289 | Incline, etc. | 1825 |
| LOW LAMBTON | 78/320546 | Viaduct | 1838 |
| MONKWEARMOUTH | | Station | 1848 |
| NORTH LEAZES | 85/175276 | Earthworks | 1825 |
| PITTINGTON | 58/324458 | Inclines | 1831 |
| SEAHAM | 85/431493 | Incline | 1828 |
| TANFIELD LEA | 78/205562 | Bridge | 1727 |
| WARDEN LAW | 85/369500 | Inclines, etc. | 1822+ |

ESSEX

| | | | |
|---|---|---|---|
| AUDLEY END | 148/513388 | Tunnels | 1844 |
| CHAPPEL | 149/895275 | Viaduct | 1849 |
| COLCHESTER | | Station | 1846 |

GLOUCESTERSHIRE (Gloucs)

| | | | |
|---|---|---|---|
| BRISTOL | Queens Road | Museum; Railway Exhibits | |
| | Temple Meads | Station | 1841+ |
| BULLO PILL | 156/689100 | Earthworks | 1810 |
| CANNOP | 142/608116 | Earthworks | 1810 |
| CHELTENHAM SPA | Lansdowne | Station | 1840 |

| | | | |
|---|---|---|---|
| CINDERFORD BRIDGE | | Earthworks, etc. | 1809 |
| DARK HILL | 155/595087 | Tunnel, etc. | 1810 |
| THE HAIE | 143/670101 | Tunnel | 1810 |
| LECKHAMPTON HILL | 143/951189 | Inclines | 1810 |
| MANGOTSFIELD | 156/664763 | Bridge | 1832 |
| NEWLAND | 155/549095 | Tunnel | 1812 |
| OLDLAND COMMON | 156/674712 | Tunnel | 1832 |
| PARKEND | 156/613080 | Sleepers | 1810 |
| REDBROOK | 142/537100 | Bridge and Incline | 1812 |
| SISTON | 156/690750 | Earthworks | 1832 |
| TEWKESBURY | | Museum; Tramway Relics | |
| WARMLEY | 156/671737 | Bridge and Tunnel | 1832 |
| WILLSBRIDGE | 156/660176 | Cutting and Tunnel | 1832 |

## HAMPSHIRE (Hants)

| | | | |
|---|---|---|---|
| BEAULIEU ABBEY | | Loco and Coaches Preserved | |
| GOSPORT | | Old Station | 1842 |
| LONGMOOR | 169/797313 | RCT Establishment; Working Steam Railway | |
| MICHELDEVER | 168/500380 | Earthworks | 1840 |

## HEREFORDSHIRE (Hereford)

| | | | |
|---|---|---|---|
| BISHOPSWOOD | 142/588180 | Tunnel | 1810 |
| EARDISLEY | 142/315486 | Culvert | 1820 |
| KINGTON | 129/298567 | Bridges | 1820 |
| ST DEVEREUX | 142/441310 | Earthworks | 1829 |

## HERTFORDSHIRE (Herts)

| | | | |
|---|---|---|---|
| BOXMOOR | 160/030063 | Embankment | 1837 |
| POTTERS BAR | 160/259999 | Tunnels | 1850 |
| TRING | 159/940137 | Cutting | 1837 |
| WATFORD | 160/094993 | Tunnel | 1837 |
| WELWYN | 160/237117 | Viaduct | 1850 |

## KENT

| | | | |
|---|---|---|---|
| CANTERBURY | Riding Gate | Loco Preserved | |
| DOVER | Town | Station | 1844 |
| FOLKESTONE | 173/227366 | Viaduct | 1843 |
| SHAKESPEARE CLIFF | 173/303397 | Sea Wall, etc. | 1843 |
| STROOD | 172/728711 | Tunnel | 1824 |
| TENTERDEN | Station | Locos Preserved | |
| TYLER HILL | 173/143597 | Tunnel | 1829 |

## LANCASHIRE (Lancs)

| | | | |
|---|---|---|---|
| CHAT MOSS | 101/700972 | Roadbed | 1830 |
| CROOKE | 100/552074 | Trace | 1812 |
| EARLESTOWN | 100/569947 | Viaduct | 1830 |
| GATHURST | 100/543075 | Incline | 1776 |
| HORWICH | | Loco Works | 1886 |
| LANCASTER | Penny Street | Old Station | 1840 |
| LIVERPOOL | Edge Hill | Tunnels | 1829 |
| | Lime Street | Cutting | 1829 |
| | William Brown Street | Museum; Railway Exhibits | |
| MANCHESTER | Ducie Street | Warehouse | 1865 |
| | Liverpool Road | Station, etc. | 1830 |
| NEWTON-LE-WILLOWS | 100/591954 | Viaduct | 1830 |
| RAINHILL | 100/490914 | Bridge | 1830 |
| STOCKPORT | 101/891904 | Viaduct | 1841 |
| WHALLEY | 95/728360 | Viaduct | 1848 |

## LEICESTERSHIRE (Leics)

| Place | Location | Relic | Date |
|---|---|---|---|
| ASHBY-DE-LA-ZOUCH | The Callis | Bridge | 1802 |
| | | Station | 1849 |
| | Station Yard | Tracks | 1802 |
| BELVOIR CASTLE | 113/820340 | Rails | 1815 |
| BOTTESFORD WHARF | 113/805374 | Sleepers | 1815 |
| CADEBY | 121/426023 | Working Steam Railway | |
| GLENFIELD | 121/552064 | Tunnel | 1832 |
| HEATH END | 121/359209 | Bridge | 1802 |
| LEICESTER | Newarke House | Museum; Railway Exhibits | |
| | Stoneygate | Tram Depot; Locos Preserved | |
| OLD PARKS | 121/363185 | Tunnel | 1802 |
| WILLESLEY | 121/340147 | Earthworks | 1802 |

## LINCOLNSHIRE (Lincs)

| Place | Location | Relic | Date |
|---|---|---|---|
| SKEGNESS | Butlins Holiday Camp | Locos Preserved | |

## LONDON

| Place | Location | Relic | Date |
|---|---|---|---|
| BATTERSEA | | Bridge | 1865 |
| BLACKFRIARS | | Bridge | 1868 |
| | | Station Entrance | 1886 |
| BRICKLAYERS ARMS | | Station | 1840 |
| BROAD STREET | | Station and Depot | 1866 |
| CAMDEN TOWN | | Engine Shed | 1837 |
| CANNON STREET | | Bridge | 1866 |
| CHARING CROSS | | Bridge | 1864 |
| | | Hotel | 1864 |
| CLAPHAM (HIGH STREET) | Museum | Major Railway Exhibits | |
| DULWICH COLLEGE | | Bridges | 1862 |
| FENCHURCH STREET | | Station | 1853+ |
| FULHAM | Lillie Bridge | LT Depot, Locos in Steam | |
| KENSINGTON | Exhibition Road | Museum; Railway Exhibits | |
| KINGS CROSS | | Station | 1852 |
| KING WILLIAM STREET | | Tunnel | 1890 |
| LONDON BRIDGE | | Viaduct | 1836 |
| NEASDEN | LT Depot | Locos in Steam | |
| PADDINGTON | | Station | 1854 |
| PRIMROSE HILL | | Tunnel | 1837 |
| ST PANCRAS | | Station | 1868 |
| | | Hotel | 1876 |
| TOWER | | Tunnel | 1870 |
| VICTORIA | | Bridge | 1867 |
| WAPPING | | Tunnel Shaft | 1843 |
| WIMBLEDON | Summerstown Road | Trace | 1805 |

## MIDDLESEX (Msx)

| Place | Location | Relic | Date |
|---|---|---|---|
| HANWELL | 160/150804 | Viaduct | 1838 |

## NORFOLK

| Place | Location | Relic | Date |
|---|---|---|---|
| BRESSINGHAM HALL | 136/079807 | Working Steam Railways | |

## NORTHAMPTONSHIRE (Northants)

| Place | Location | Relic | Date |
|---|---|---|---|
| HARRINGWORTH | 133/915975 | Viaduct | 1878 |
| KETTERING | | Station | 1857 |
| KILSBY | 133/570707 | Tunnel | 1837 |
| PETERBOROUGH | 134/191981 | Bridge | 1850 |
| ROADE | 146/750523 | Cutting | 1838 |

## NORTHUMBERLAND (Nthmb)

| Place | Location | Relic | Date |
|---|---|---|---|
| BARDON MILL | 77/777645 | Station | 1836 |

| | | | |
|---|---|---|---|
| BLYTHE | Horton Bridge | Earthworks | c1709 |
| HEXHAM | | Station | 1836 |
| NEWCASTLE | 78/252637 | Bridge | 1849 |
| | Central | Station | 1850+ |
| | Exhibition Park | Museum; Railway Exhibits | |
| STOCKSFIELD | 78/054613 | Station | 1836 |
| WILLINGTON QUAY | 78/324669 | Earthworks | 1820 |
| WYLAM | 78/119646 | Station | 1836 |

## NOTTINGHAMSHIRE (Notts)

| | | | |
|---|---|---|---|
| MANSFIELD | Museum | Tramway Exhibits | |
| NEW BRINSLEY | 112/460500 | Bridge | 1817 |

## RUTLAND *see* Northants

## SHROPSHIRE (Salop)

| | | | |
|---|---|---|---|
| BRIDGNORTH | | Working Steam Railway | |
| BUILDWAS | 119/662038 | Bridge | 1863 |
| COALBROOKDALE | Darby Road | Private Museum; Tramway Exhibits | |
| LLANYMYNECH | 117/265215 | Incline, etc. | 1800 |
| LLYNCLYS | 118/285241 | Earthworks | c1800 |
| PANT | 117/277224 | Bridge | c1800 |
| PEN-Y-FOEL | 117/260217 | Inclines | c1794 |
| WHARF HOUSE | 130/672705 | Tramway Remains | 1796 |

## SOMERSET (Somt)

| | | | |
|---|---|---|---|
| BATH | 166/766624 | Incline | 1755 |
| | Green Park | Station | 1870 |
| | Spa | Station | 1841 |
| BLEADON AND UPHILL STATION | 165/325578 | Loco Preserved | |
| MINEHEAD | Butlins Holiday Camp | Loco Preserved | |
| RADSTOCK | 166/692550 | Earthworks | 1815 |
| SINGLE HILL | 166/720561 | Earthworks | 1815 |
| UPHILL | 165/326581 | Bridge | 1841 |
| WELLOW | 166/740582 | Tunnel | 1815 |
| WELTON | 166/670551 | Sleepers | 1815 |

## STAFFORDSHIRE (Staffs)

| | | | |
|---|---|---|---|
| DILHORNE | 110/977444 | Working Steam Railway | |
| FROGHALL | 111/028477 | Inclines | 1777 |
| HARECASTLE | 110/845526 | Tunnels | 1848 |
| HOFTEN'S CROSS | 111/072480 | Earthworks | 1802 |
| SHUGBOROUGH | 119/975216 | Tunnel | 1847 |
| | 119/992224 | Museum; Railway Exhibits | |
| STOKE-ON-TRENT | | Station and Square | 1848 |
| TRUBSHAW | 110/858550 | Sleepers, etc. | c1817 |
| UPPER COTTON | 111/055480 | Incline | 1777 |
| WETLEY ROCKS | 110/968486 | Bridge | c1780 |
| WHISTON | 111/029476 | Bridge, etc. | 1802 |

## SUFFOLK

| | | | |
|---|---|---|---|
| NEWMARKET | | Old Station | 1848 |

## SURREY

| | | | |
|---|---|---|---|
| COULSDON | 170/296595 | Earthworks | 1805 |
| CROYDON | Avon Path | Trace | 1805 |
| | Waterworks Square | Pumping House | c1844 |
| MERSTHAM | 170/289550 | Tunnel, etc. | 1805 |

| | | | |
|---|---|---|---|
| MERSTHAM | 170/288558 | Bridge Remains | 1805 |
| | 170/286511 | Building | 1805 |
| | 170/288545 | Building | 1805 |
| PURLEY | 170/316622 | Rails | 1805 |
| **SUSSEX** | | | |
| BALCOMBE | 182/323278 | Viaduct | 1840 |
| BATTLE | | Station | 1852 |
| BRIGHTON | 182/309057 | Viaduct | 1846 |
| | Paston Place | Electric Railway | 1883 |
| | | Station | 1841 |
| CLAYTON | 182/296130 | Tunnel | 1841 |
| SHEFFIELD PARK STATION | 183/404237 | Working Steam Railway | |
| **WARWICKSHIRE** | | | |
| ALDERMINSTER | 142/230487 | Bridges, etc. | 1826 |
| BERRY FIELD FARM | 144/221452 | Earthworks | 1826 |
| BIRMINGHAM | Curzon Street | Station | 1838 |
| | Newhall Street | Museum; Railway Exhibits | |
| STRATFORD-ON-AVON | 142/425548 | Bridge and Tramway Relics | 1826 |
| TARTON | 144/242473 | Bridge | 1826 |
| WARWICK | Milverton | Station | 1844 |
| **WILTSHIRE (Wilts)** | | | |
| BOX | 156/843692 | Tunnel | 1841 |
| CHIPPENHAM | 157/960777 | Viaduct | 1839 |
| MIDDLEHILL | 156/820688 | Tunnel | 1841 |
| SWINDON | Faringdon Street | Railway Museum | |
| | | Railway Town, etc. | 1843+ |
| **WORCESTERSHIRE (Worcs)** | | | |
| GREAT MALVERN | | Station | 1859 |
| **YORKSHIRE (Yorks)** | | | |
| BLEA MOOR | 90/769870 | Tunnel | 1875 |
| DEWSBURY | Staincliffe Road | Sleepers | 1805 |
| FLOCKTON | 96/250160 | Viaduct | 1773 |
| GOATHLAND | 92/832013 | Incline | 1836 |
| HAW | 96/000530 | Bridges | 1786 |
| HAWORTH | | Working Steam Railway | |
| HUDDERSFIELD | | Station | 1847 |
| HULL | Paragon | Station | 1848 |
| | High Street | Transport Museum | |
| LEEDS | 96/305312 | Staithes | 1758 |
| | Moor Lane | Working Steam Railway | |
| | Old Run Road | Incline | 1758 |
| LITTLEBOROUGH | 95/944194 | Tunnel | 1839 |
| LITTLE SMEATON | 103/531164 | Earthworks | c1827 |
| ROCKLEY AND BROOM ROYD | 102/330020 | Earthworks, etc. | 1820 |
| SCARBOROUGH | | Station | 1845 |
| SHADE | 95/930231 | Bridge | 1838 |
| SILKSTONE | 102/291059 | Sleepers, etc. | 1809 |
| STANDEDGE | 102/025100 | Tunnel | 1849 |
| TODMORDEN | 95/954246 | Viaduct | 1839 |
| WOODHEAD | 102/135011 | Tunnel | 1845 |
| WORSBOROUGH BRIDGE | 102/365035 | Bridge | 1820 |
| YORK | Queen Street | Old Station | 1841 |
| | Queen Street | Railway Museum | |
| | | Station | 1877 |

# SCOTLAND

| | | | |
|---|---|---|---|
| **ANGUS** | | | |
| DUNDEE | 50/394275 | Bridge | 1887 |
| **AYRSHIRE** | | | |
| AYR | Butlins Holiday Camp | Loco Preserved | |
| BALLOCHMYLE | 67/480329 | Viaduct | 1848 |
| DRYBRIDGE | 67/359364 | Bridge | 1812 |
| FAIRLIE | 67/383369 | Bridge | 1812 |
| FERGUSHILL | 59/326432 | Bridge | 1831 |
| NETHER MAINS | 59/308422 | Bridge | 1831 |
| **CLACKMANNAN** | | | |
| ALLOA | Castle Street | Bridges | 1768 |
| **EAST LOTHIAN** | | | |
| CLIFTON HALL | 62/110714 | Viaduct | 1841 |
| COCKENZIE | 62/399757 | Sleepers | 1813 |
| EDINBURGH | Haymarket | Tunnel | 1841 |
| | Scotland Street | Tunnel | 1847 |
| | | Museum; Railway Exhibits | |
| PRESTONPANS | 62/399749 | Causeway | 1722 |
| **FIFE** | | | |
| BURNTISLAND | Starleyburn | Incline, etc. | c1817 |
| CROSSGATES | 55/145887 | Tunnel | 1833 |
| DUNFERMLINE | Quarry | Inclines | 1821 |
| HALBEATH | 55/126887 | Bridge | 1780 |
| LOCHTY | 56/522080 | Working Steam Railway | |
| QUEENSFERRY | 62/135795 | Bridge | 1890 |
| **INVERNESS-SHIRE** | | | |
| GLENFINNAN | 35/910813 | Viaduct | 1898 |
| **RENFREWSHIRE** | | | |
| GLASGOW | Albert Drive | Transport Museum | |
| | Queen Street | Station | 1842+ |
| ROBROYSTON | 60/628695 | Embankment | 1831 |
| **STIRLING** | | | |
| KINNAIRD | 55/869851 | Trace | 1760 |
| **(BERWICK-ON-TWEED)** | | | |
| BERWICK | 64/992530 | Bridge | 1850 |

# WALES

| | | | |
|---|---|---|---|
| **ANGLESEY** | | | |
| MENAI BRIDGE | 107/542710 | Bridge | 1850 |
| **BRECKNOCKSHIRE (Brecon)** | | | |
| ABERCRAVE | 153/815126 | Incline | 1798 |
| BRYNMAWR | 141/195127 | Bridge | 1795 |
| COLLWNG VALLEY | 141/120180 | Trace | 1815 |
| DAREN | 141/205162 | Sleepers | c1816 |
| GILWERN | 141/241150 | Bridge | 1795 |
| HAY | The Warren | Earthworks | 1817 |
| | Station | Bridge | 1817 |
| TAL-Y-LLYN | 141/105276 | Tunnel | 1817 |
| WERN WATKIN | 141/215154 | Incline | c1816 |
| YNNYS-CEDWYN | 153/784095 | Incline | 1834 |

## CAERNARVONSHIRE (Caern)

| | | | |
|---|---|---|---|
| BANGOR | | Station | 1848 |
| BONTNEWYDD | 107/480599 | Bridge Remains | 1828 |
| CAERNARVON | Afon Seiont | Bridge Remains | 1828 |
| | Coed Helen | Tunnel | 1828 |
| CONWAY | 107/987776 | Bridge | 1849 |
| | | Station | 1848 |
| GARTH | 107/549680 | Incline | 1824 |
| LLANBERIS | | Working Steam Railway | |
| NANTLLE | 107/509534 | Bridge | 1828 |
| PENRHYN CASTLE | 107/602719 | Railway Exhibits | |
| PORTMADOC | | Working Steam Railway | |
| | | Causeway | 1811 |
| PORT PENRHYN | 107/610680 | Bridge | 1801 |
| PWLLHELI | Butlins Holiday Camp | Loco Preserved | |

## CARDIGANSHIRE (Card)

| | | | |
|---|---|---|---|
| ABERYSTWYTH | | Working Steam Railway | |

## CARMARTHENSHIRE (Carm)

| | | | |
|---|---|---|---|
| CARWAY | 152/465065 | Bridge | c1802 |
| DAFEN | 153/532011 | Incline | 1833 |

## DENBIGHSHIRE (Denb)

| | | | |
|---|---|---|---|
| HENDY | 117/200446 | Incline | c1852 |
| PONT-CYSYLLTE | 117/273425 | Bridges | 1806 |
| TREVOR | 117/242423 | Tramway Remains | c1806 |

## FLINTSHIRE (Flint)

| | | | |
|---|---|---|---|
| ASTON HALL | 109/315673 | Earthworks | c1801 |
| DANIELS ASH | 109/318663 | Earthworks | c1801 |
| FLINT | | Station | 1848 |
| HOLYWELL | | Station | 1848 |

## GLAMORGAN (Glam)

| | | | |
|---|---|---|---|
| ABERDARE | Canal Basin | Sleepers | 1817 |
| BIRCHGROVE | 153/707984 | Earthworks | 1816 |
| CARDIFF | Museum | Railway Exhibits | |
| CASTLE MORLAIS | 154/047098 | Sleepers | 1803 |
| CEFN MORFUDD | 153/790170 | Inclines | c1810 |
| CFFN-COED-Y-CYMMER | 154/033081 | Sleepers | 1792 |
| CYMFRTHFA | 154/041083 | Bridge | 1792 |
| CYMAVON | 153/787923 | Bridge | 1819 |
| EDWARDSVILLE | 154/082968 | Bridge | 1815 |
| HIRWAUN | 154/955055 | Causeway | 1794 |
| LLWYDCOED | 154/984044 | Bridge, etc. | 1805 |
| MERTHYR VALE | 154/074000 | Sleepers | 1802 |
| MYNYDD BYCHAN | 153/794926 | Incline | 1819 |
| MYNYDD FFORCH-DWN | 153/824978 | Inclines | c1810 |
| PONTNEDDFECHAN | 154/900077 | Sleepers | c1810 |
| PONT-RHYD-Y-FEN | 153/797941 | Earthworks | c1824 |
| RESOLVEN | 153/830027 | Sleepers | 1837 |
| ROBERTSTOWN | 154/003033 | Bridge | 1817 |
| SWANSEA | Victoria Road | Museum; Railway Exhibits | |
| TONDU | 154/894843 | Bridge, etc. | 1828+ |
| TONMAWR | 153/804963 | Bridges | c1815 |
| WENALLT WOOD | 153/785992 | Incline | c1810 |

## MERIONETHSHIRE (Merioneth)

| | | | |
|---|---|---|---|
| BARMOUTH | 116/623150 | Viaduct | 1867 |
| BOSTON LODGE | 116/585379 | Workshops | 1836 |

| | | | |
|---|---|---|---|
| PENRHYNDEUDRAETH | 116/619383 | Bridge | 1867 |
| TAN-Y-BWLCH | 116/650416 | Trace, etc. | 1836 |
| TOWYN | Wharf Station | Narrow Gauge Museum<br>Working Steam Railway | |

MONTGOMERYSHIRE (Montgomery)

| | | | |
|---|---|---|---|
| HILL HOUSE FARM | 129/297689 | Sleepers | 1820 |
| WELSHPOOL | | Working Steam Railway | |

PEMBROKESHIRE (Pembs)

| | | | |
|---|---|---|---|
| KILGETTY | 152/126072 | Bridge | 1842 |
| SAUNDERSFOOT | 152/137047 | Tunnel, etc. | 1832 |
| WISEMANS BRIDGE | 152/145060 | Tunnels | 1842 |

(MONMOUTHSHIRE) (Mon)

| | | | |
|---|---|---|---|
| BLAENAVON | Prince Street | Bridge | 1795 |
| CHEPSTOW | 156/539941 | Bridge Remains | 1852 |
| CROSSKEYS | 154/217915 | Bridge | 1824 |
| PANDY | 142/335225 | Earthworks | 1818 |
| PONTHIR | 155/324928 | Bridge, etc. | c1801 |
| PONTLLANFRAITH | 154/175961 | Sleepers | 1824 |
| PONTYMOILE | Victoria Road | Sleepers | 1795 |
| PONTYPOOL | The Grove | Tunnel | 1829 |
| PWLLDU | 154/248114 | Tunnel | 1815 |
| SUDBROOK | 155/525865 | Tunnel | 1886 |

# List of Engineers, Architects, etc.


Adams, J., 86
Adams, W., 97
Allen, A., 81
Andrews, G., 71, 72
Aspinall, J., 84, 98

Baker, B., 60
Barlow, P., 55
Barlow, W., 59, 60
Barnes, F., 71
Barry, C., 62
Barry, E., 68
Beattie, W., 83, 104
Beaumont, H., 15, 26
Birkinshaw, J., 44
Bonomi, I., 47
Bouch, T., 55, 60
Brandling, C., 19
Bruff, P., 55
Brunel, I., 49, 52, 54, 56, 58, 59, 62, 64, 70, 112
Bulleid, O., 88, 104
Bury, E., 81

Churchward, G., 80, 100
Clark, T., 104
Collett, C., 86, 97, 100
Crossley, J., 55
Cubitt, L., 67
Cubitt, W., 54

Darby, A., 21
Dean, J., 84
Dogson, J., 70
Drummond, D., 83, 84, 89
Drummond, P., 85

Edmundson, T., 115

Fairbairn, J., 57
Fletcher, E., 80, 83, 96
Foster, J., 63, 80
Fowler, H., 60, 86, 87, 99
Fowler, J., 59

Greathead, J., 59
Green, B., 54
Gresley, N., 87, 96, 98, 192, 104

Hackworth, T., 79, 81
Hardwick, P., 66, 68
Hawkshaw, J., 59
Heywood, T., 86
Hedley, W., 46, 79
Holden, J., 84, 85, 104
Holmes, M., 101

Ivatt, H., 84, 85, 88, 98, 100, 104

James, W., 40, 44, 51
Jessop, J., 41
Jessop, W., 24, 27, 30, 34
Johnson, S., 84, 85, 98

Kirtley, M., 82

Locke, J., 53, 54

Maunsell, R., 86
McIntosh, J., 84
Mocatta, D., 52, 67

Outram, B., 22, 24, 28

Parks, J., 97
Paxton, J., 69
Pritchett, J., 71
Proser, T., 72

Ramsbottom, J., 82
Rastrick, J., 41, 51, 55, 80
Rennie, J., 25
Robinson, J., 85, 86

Scott, G., 73, 74
Stanier, W., 87
Stephenson, G., 32, 47, 50, 54, 80
Stephenson, R., 51, 56, 58
Stirling, P., 83
Stroudley, W., 83, 97

Thompson, B., 46
Thompson, F., 58, 68, 69
Tite, W., 69, 70
Tress, W., 69
Trevithick, R., 46, 59
Trevithick, W., 82

Vignoles, C., 52
Volk, M., 111

Wainwright, H., 85, 97, 101
Webb, F., 84, 116
Whitelegg, R., 85
Wood, J., 17
Wood, R., 16
Wood, S., 67
Worsdell, W., 84
Wyatt, M., 65, 68